Classics

MANCHESTER CITY

FOOTBALL CLUB

Not a classic match but a classic moment in the history of Manchester City Football Club. Contrary to popular belief, the result of the game did not send City's neighbours down, but it certainly put a smile on the faces of City supporters, and left many Reds with a broken heart as they travelled on their various journeys home to the four corners of the UK!

To all City supporters, young and old, who were lucky,
or not so lucky in some instances, to witness these unforgettable matches.

Classics

MANCHESTER CITY
FOOTBALL CLUB

ANDREW WALDON & DAVID SAFFER

TEMPUS

First published 2001
Copyright © Andrew Waldon & David Saffer, 2001

Tempus Publishing Limited
The Mill, Brimscombe Port,
Stroud, Gloucestershire, GL5 2QG

ISBN 0 7524 2255 3

Typesetting and origination by
Tempus Publishing Limited
Printed in Great Britain by
Midway Colour Print, Wiltshire

ACKNOWLEDGEMENTS

We would like to thank all of the following individuals and organizations for their help with this publication: Tony Book, Roy Clarke, Bert Trautmann, Ken Barnes, Roy Little, Johnny Williamson, Paddy Fagan, Paul Power; Gary James, John Rowan, Bernadetta Cummings for the proof reading, and James Howarth at Tempus Publishing.

While every attempt has been made to acknowledge the original source of copyright for all pictures in this book, if anyone has any questions relating to this matter please contact the publishers.

Andrew Waldon

David Saffer

INTRODUCTION

There have been numerous books on Manchester City Football Club, but to our knowledge only one, *Blue Heaven*, has ever covered specific matches, and in this publication, just twelve games were recollected through the eyes of a number of ex-legends. We decided to expand on the theme and cover seventy matches with player quotes and relevant memorabilia pertaining to the game itself. So, how do you define a *classic* football match – legendary, memorable, outstanding, unforgettable? All or a mixture of the above could apply to each or any of the games in this book.

Writing *City Classics* has been fantastic, apart from deciding on the actual matches to be included, which at times seemed nigh on impossible, because we knew that if you had one hundred City supporters in a room, each would select a different set of matches. However, having completed our task, we are confident that each would have many of the matches we have included in their list.

What we have endeavoured to include is a variety of games spanning the entire history of the club, from Ardwick FC to Manchester City FC, over a period in excess of 100 incredible years. *City Classics* recalls the highs and the lows, the routine, and the idiosyncratic. We re-live the successes of City's First Division championship-winning seasons; the FA Cup, League Cup, and European triumphs; the rise in recent seasons from Division Two mediocrity to the promised land of the Premiership; and, finally, last season's fall from top-flight football once again.

There are so many unforgettable games that, together, they create a collective memory of this great club. We are sure that when you have finished reading this book, you will say, 'why did they omit this game or that game?'.

We hope you derive as much pleasure from reading *City Classics* as we have done from researching and writing it.

Andrew Waldon & David Saffer
November 2001

FOREWORD

Thinking about past matches involving Manchester City has always been enjoyable for me, because I was fortunate to take part in so many unforgettable games.

During my time I played, managed, scouted for and coached the youths, reserve and first teams and have no regrets about the time I spent at Maine Road. The period 1967-1970 was a particularly pleasing one for the club and for me as it was the time when City found great success; winning the FA Cup, the League Cup and the European Cup Winners Cup.

I am sure you will enjoy reliving those moments. As a player the highlight for me has to be the championship decider at Newcastle in 1968. I had always measured my own performance on consistency over a period of time and to win the championship was something special. The highlight for me as a manager was undoubtedly the 1976 League Cup Final when we beat Newcastle.

I am convinced the quality and quantity of this publication will disappoint no fan. I hope that the pages that follow give every reader a thorough understanding of what its like to be a City fan and what the club have achieved over more than a century of football.

I am sure Kevin Keegan and his staff will be doing their utmost to give the fans more of what they want: 'Classic City'. The fans deserve something and have been terrific over the years.

Enjoy this book, it really will bring back the memories.

Tony Book.

THE 70 CLASSIC MATCHES

3 September 1892 Ardwick v. Bootle
First football League match
17 March 1894 Small Heath v. Ardwick
Heaviest defeat in League football, 2-10
3 November 1894 Manchester City v. Newton Heath
First League meeting between both Manchester clubs and also the introduction of Billy Meredith
23 March 1895 Manchester City v. Lincoln City
11-3 victory
18 February 1899 Manchester City v. Darwen
City win promotion for the first time, winning 10-0. F. Williams scores 5, being the first player to do so
9 September 1899 Manchester City v. Derby County
First home game in top flight
14 April 1903 Barnsley v. Manchester City
City clinch title and promotion for the second time
23 April 1904 Manchester City v. Bolton Wanderers
City's first FA Cup final
1 September 1906 Manchester City v. Woolwich Arsenal
City finish game with six players
3 September 1906 Everton v. Manchester City
1-9 record Division One defeat
23 April 1910 Manchester City v. Leeds City
City clinch title and promotion for the third time
20 April 1921 Manchester City v. Preston North End
City finish as runners up in the First Division
25 August 1923 Manchester City v. Sheffield United
Opening game at Maine Road
24 October 1925 Manchester City v. Burnley
City are relegated. Browell scores five – the first City player to do so in the First Division. Team lets in 100 goals
20 February 1926 Manchester City v. Crystal Palace
Record FA Cup win 11-4. Roberts scores five
24 April 1926 Manchester City v. Bolton Wanderers
FA Cup final
7 May 1927 Manchester City v. Bradford City
City are pipped for promotion, despite winning 8-0
30 January 1929 Manchester City v. Bury
6-4 win. Tommy Johnson scores two. His 38 goals for the season is a club record
29 January 1930 Manchester City v. Swindon Town
FA Cup win 10-1. Marshall scores five
29 April 1933 Manchester City v. Everton
City lose FA Cup final
3 March 1934 Manchester City v. Stoke City
Record attendance
28 April 1934 Manchester City v. Portsmouth
City win FA Cup
24 April 1937 Manchester City v. Sheffield Wednesday
City win First Division Championship
26 December 1938 Tranmere Rovers v. Manchester City
9-3 win
27 December 1938 Manchester City v. Tranmere Rovers
Return next day, 5-2 win
24 May 1947 Manchester City v. West Ham United
Revenge and victory assured City of the Second Division championship
21 August 1954 Preston North End v. Manchester City
First game under Revie plan, lost 0-5

12 February 1955 Manchester United v. Manchester City
City beat United three times in a season, including 5-0 away
26 March 1955 Manchester City v. Sunderland
FA Cup semi-final
7 May 1955 Manchester City v. Newcastle United
FA Cup final, City lose 1-3
5 May 1956 Manchester City v. Birmingham City
City win FA Cup final
9 January 1957 Manchester City v. Newcastle United
City lose 4-5
21 September 1957 West Bromwich Albion v. Manchester City
2-9 defeat, City finish fifth. They score 104 and concede 100
28 January 1961 Luton Town v. Manchester City
Denis Law scores six goals and the game is abandoned
3 March 1962 Manchester City v. Tottenham Hotspur
City defeat defending Double winners 6-2
16 January 1965 Manchester City v. Swindon Town
Lowest ever home League crowd
13 May 1966 Charlton Athletic v. Manchester City
First Mercer/Allison triumph, promotion
9 December 1967 Manchester City v. Tottenham Hotspur
Ballet on ice
31 January 1968 Reading v. Manchester City
7-0 to City following draw at Maine Road
11 May 1968 Newcastle United v. Manchester City
City win Championship
18 September 1968 Manchester City v. Fenerbahce SK
City's first European game
7 December 1968 Manchester City v. Burnley
7-0 – biggest League win in Mercer/Allison reign
26 April 1969 Leicester City v. Manchester City
City win FA Cup
15 November 1969 Manchester City v. Manchester United
4-0, one of three wins in the season for the second time in club's history
7 March 1970 Manchester City v. West Bromwich Albion
City win League Cup
29 April 1970 Manchester City v. Gornik Zabrze
City win European Cup Winners Cup
2 March 1974 Manchester City v. Wolverhampton Wanderers
League Cup final
28 February 1976 Manchester City v. Newcastle United
City win Football League Cup
26 November 1977 Manchester City v. Chelsea
6-2, Tueart scores three, one of three hat-tricks in a season
23 November 78 AC Milan v. Manchester City
Memorable European night played twenty-four hours after it should have been due to fog
5 January 1980 Halifax Town v. Manchester City
Famous defeat in FA Cup
14 January 1981 Manchester City v. Liverpool
League Cup semi-final, hotly disputed goal prevents City from appearing in final
11 April 1981 Manchester City v. Ipswich Town
FA Cup semi-final, City are underdogs but win
9 May 1981 Manchester City v. Tottenham Hotspur
The centenary FA Cup final…
14 May 1981 Tottenham Hotspur v. Manchester City
…and its memorable replay

5 September 1981 Stoke City *v.* Manchester City
First appearance of Trevor Francis and an amazing away following
14 May 1983 Manchester City *v.* Luton Town
Relegation confirmed in the last few minutes
23 March 1986 Manchester City *v.* Chelsea
Full Members Cup final, City losing 1-5, finishes 4-5
7 November 1987 Manchester City *v.* Huddersfield Town
City's record score and three individual hat-tricks
27 August 1988 Hull City *v.* Manchester City
Start of the inflatable craze
13 May 1989 Bradford City *v.* Manchester City
City claim automatic promotion
23 September 1989 Manchester City *v.* Manchester United
Famous 5-1 victory
20 April 1991 Manchester City *v.* Derby County
'Keeper Tony Coton is sent off, goalscoring hero Niall Quinn goes in goal and saves a penalty
17 August 1992 Manchester City *v.* Queens Park Rangers
First ever Monday night live Sky game
22 October 1994 Manchester City *v.* Tottenham Hotspur
Classic seven-goal thriller in front of television cameras
19 August 1998 Manchester City *v.* Notts County
Record win in Worthington Cup, 7-1
8 December 1998 Manchester City *v.* Mansfield Town
First ever appearance in Auto Windscreen Cup, lowest crowd
20 March 1999 Colchester United *v.* Manchester City
First pay-per-view game and the reality of Division Two football
30 May 1999 Manchester City *v.* Gillingham
Play-off final
7 May 2000 Blackburn Rovers *v.* Manchester City
City clinch promotion back to the Premiership
5 September 2000 Leeds United *v.* Manchester City
City's remarkable progress
7 May 2001 Ipswich Town *v.* Manchester City
Relegation

ROLL OF HONOUR

Football League Division One champions
1936/37, 1967/68
Division Two champions
1898/99, 1902/03, 1909/10, 1927/28, 1946/47, 1965/66
Division Two Play-off winners
1998/99
European Cup-Winners Cup winners
1969/70
FA Cup winners
1904, 1934, 1956, 1969
Football League Cup winners
1970, 1976
FA Charity Shield winners
1937/38, 1968/69, 1972/73
FA Youth Cup winners
1986

ARDWICK V. BOOTLE

3 September 1892

Football League Second Division
Hyde Road, Manchester
Attendance: 4,000

Ardwick 7   Bootle 0
Davies (3)
Morris (2)
Weir, Angus

In 1892, Ardwick Association Football Club made a significant move towards their ultimate aim of being one of the country's elite teams. A decision had been made to form the Second Division of the Football League and Ardwick's application was accepted.

The Brewerymen, as they were called at the time, made their debut in the Football League at home to Bootle. The day itself was particularly grey, with rain falling throughout nearly the whole of the match, and the poor conditions kept the attendance down.

Jack Angus started the game for Ardwick with some good forward play, and he was well supported by Dave Russell. Their next attack saw Joe Davies receive a pass from William Hopkins and, with only McLaughlin to beat, his finishing was of poor quality. Ardwick continued to apply the pressure and, in another attack, William Douglas found Hugh Morris in a good attacking position. He passed to Davies, who rounded a Bootle defender and saw his shot strike the upright. Ardwick were then awarded a penalty for a foul on Angus, but Russell's spot kick went straight into the hands of McLaughlin. Shortly afterwards, Morris had the distinction of scoring the club's first goal in the League. From this point up until the interval, the play could best be described as one-sided. Davies scored the second and fourth goals and, in between, H. Middleton scored, although this was later credited to Davie Weir, and Angus added a fifth just before the half time break.

The pattern of the second half followed that of the first, and Ardwick completely swamped the Bootle goal, Morris eventually scoring a sixth goal. Bootle did manage a momentary visit into the Ardwick half, and Douglas was tested by a shot from Finlayson. However, this was merely a brief respite, and the Bootle goal subsequently had several lucky escapes, McLaughlin, in particular, saving well from Weir. It was not long before the seventh and final goal of the game arrived, Davies completing the first Ardwick League hat-trick as a result of good play by Bob Milarvie.

Bootle had been inferior in all departments and were decisively beaten. The comprehensive victory put City at the top of the Second Division, and they eventually finished fifth, with Small Heath crowned as champions.

Ardwick: Douglas, McVickers, Robson, Middleton, Russell, Hopkins, Davies, Morris, Angus, Weir, Milarvie

Bootle: McLaughlin, Hutchinson, Arridge, Neilson, Hughes, Grierson, Finlayson, Gallacher, Law, McLafferty, Montgomery

Season: 1892/93

P	W	D	L	F	A	PTS
22	9	3	10	45	40	21

Division:	Two
Position:	Fifth
Manager:	Lawrence Furniss
Top Goalscorer:	Davie Weir (8)
Average Attendance:	3,000

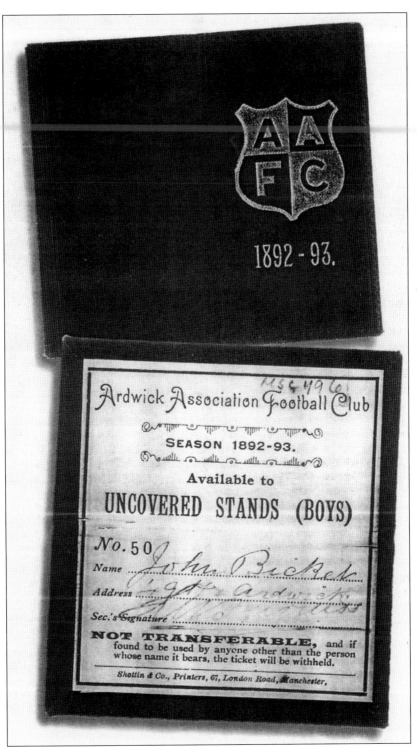

1892/93 season ticket.

SMALL HEATH v. ARDWICK

17 March 1894

Football League Second Division
Birmingham
Attendance: 2,000

Small Heath 10   Ardwick 2
Wheldon (2), Hallam (2)   *Bennett, Robertson*
Mobley (3)
Hands, Jenkyns, Walton

For the start of the season, Ardwick replaced the much-respected figure of club secretary Lawrence Furniss with Joshua Parlby. Parlby had held a similar position at Stoke City and was thought to be the person to lead the club in the right direction.

The season, however, did not quite go in the direction that was hoped for, and there was a series of dreadful results, including a 10-2 mauling at the hands of Small Heath.

Ardwick started the game with only ten men and, right from the start, had to play on the defensive. Stand-in 'keeper Fred Steele had already made two splendid saves, before Wheldon got through and scored. The absentee, Harry Stones, finally arrived and took over as goalkeeper. Hallam then added a second goal, before Ardwick lost Jack Hargreaves, who was forced to retire from the game with an injury. The home forwards capitalized on the advantage of having an extra man and, through an excellent interchange of passes, scored a third goal, Mobley converting. Jenkyns then added a fourth, as Small Heath continued to press forward and, by the interval, they were leading 4-0.

The resumption of the second half saw an even more one-sided game, and Ardwick did not have the best of things. Their defence was under constant pressure, and the smarter, and more accurate, efforts of Small Heath led to an increase in the scoreline, as their hard work was rewarded with an additional six goals. Mobley readily accepted the chances that came his way and brought his personal tally for the game to three goals. The Ardwick defence was breached on further occasions as Wheldon, Hallam, Hands and Walton brought the Small Heath tally to double figures. When the game did take a turn in favour of Ardwick, they did manage to register two goals and gain some sort of consolation from the encounter.

The terrible run of results and falling attendances meant that the club was being hit from all directions and, after being forced to sell some of its best players, many felt they should just play out the season and call it a day. However, this was not to be countenanced, and the following season 'Manchester City' was formed.

Small Heath: Charsley, Short, Watson, Ollis, Jenkyns, Davey, Hallam, Walton, Mobley, Wheldon, Hands

Ardwick: Stones, Steele, Dyer, Bowman, Whittle, Regan, Bennett, Milne, Robertson, Hargreaves, Saddington

Season: 1893/94

P	W	D	L	F	A	PTS
28	8	2	18	47	71	18

Division:	Two
Position:	Thirteenth
Manager:	Joshua Parlby
Top Goalscorer:	Herbert Morris (7)
Average Attendance:	3,600

J. Parlby.

MANCHESTER CITY V. NEWTON HEATH

3 November 1894

Football League Second Division
Hyde Road, Manchester
Attendance: 14,000

Manchester City 2   Newton Heath 5
Meredith (2)   Smith (4)
                           Clarkin

This was the first ever League meeting between the two clubs of Manchester, and no chronicle of games would be complete without this fixture played over a hundred years ago.

Newton Heath, who later became Manchester United, had been relegated from the First Division the previous season, and were looking to return at their first attempt. Manchester City had just been accepted into the Football League.

This match also heralded the introduction of one of the greatest football legends, Billy Meredith, who was on show to the Hyde Road public for the first time.

The match was eagerly anticipated as a local derby, and it proved to be an exciting game of end-to-end football. On what was described as a dull and dismal day, Newton Heath gave City little chance and they were well beaten.

In a tense and exciting opening, Meredith raced away with the ball, but his cross was finally met by a virtually faultless Newton defence that City were finding hard to break down. James McNaught, in particular, had an outstanding game.

Richard Smith, the inside left for Newton Heath, was in irresistible form, and claimed a piece of history in this clash between the two giants of Manchester, by scoring the most goals in a single game between these sides. Once Smith had scored twice in the first thirteen minutes, City were left with an uphill battle.

City 'keeper George Hutchinson had little chance with any of the goals scored before the interval and, when City conceded further goals in the second half through John Clarkin and an additional two goals to Smith (which marked the high point of an excellent start to his first season at Newton), the game was effectively over as a contest.

Some consolation arrived for City in the goal-scoring home debut of Meredith, who later went on to play for Manchester United, when he pulled back two late goals to make the scoreline a little bit more respectable. Some sources, though, claim that James Sharples should have been accredited with one of those goals. Meredith must have been wondering what kind of club he had joined, as City had conceded ten goals in the opening two games of the season, having lost their opening game 4-5 at Newcastle United.

So Newton Heath claimed a conclusive victory, and City were convincingly beaten in front of what was their highest attendance of the season.

The return League game on 5 January 1895 saw City suffer another heavy defeat, 1-4, when James Sharples scored City's consolation.

Manchester City: Hutchinson, H. Smith, Walker, Mann, Nash, Dyer, Meredith, Finnerhan, Rowan, Sharples, Milarvie

Newton Heath: Douglas, McCartney, Erentz, Perrins, McNaught, Davidson, Clarkin, Donaldson, Dow, R. Smith, Peters

Referee: Mr Lewis (Blackburn)

Billy Meredith later recalled, 'I gave a little cheer to myself as I trotted off, and I had the satisfaction of knowing that I had made a good start in my first home match.'

Pat Finnerhan signed from Northwich Victoria and played 89 games between 1894 and 1897, scoring 27 goals.

MANCHESTER CITY V. LINCOLN CITY

23 March 1895

Football League Second Division
Hyde Road, Manchester
Attendance: 2,000

Manchester City 11   Lincoln City 3
McReddie (4)   Smallman
Rowan (3)   Lees, Walker (og)
Meredith (2)
Finnerhan, Milarvie

During this particular season, City played in a number of remarkable high-scoring games. The Blues actually finished with the highest 'goals for' record (82) but, at the same time, conceded 72. There were many extreme results, with unusual scorelines in away matches against Newcastle United (4-5), Burton Wanderers (0-8) and some incredible matches at home versus Grimsby Town (2-5), Walsall Town Swifts (6-1), Newton Heath (2-5), Notts County (7-1) and – what still stands as a club League victory, this against Lincoln City (11-3).

In that particular game, City opened the scoring within the first few minutes of play. Bob Milarvie got a clear opening and signalled his return to the side with the opening goal on three minutes. He had last played in a scoring appearance at home to Bury in a 3-3 draw, back in December of the previous year. City continued to push forward and the Lincoln defence was under severe pressure. William McReddie scored two goals in quick succession to put City further ahead, and Sandy Rowan cleverly added a fourth. Some slackness in the City defence gave Lincoln a few chances to break away. One such attack saw a sudden rush up the right wing, Smallman centred cleverly and Lees converted for Lincoln. Immediately from the restart, an excellent individual effort by Rowan raised City's total to five at the half-time interval.

City started the second half by scoring a sixth goal through McReddie. Smallman then received a good pass from Blewitt to score Lincoln's second goal of the game. Billy Meredith scored the next for City, after accepting a pass from Milarvie. The scoring continued: Rowan added an eighth, McReddie a ninth, and Meredith a tenth. In spite of this, Blewitt and Smallman made goal attempts for the visitors, and a quick centre from Smallman was diverted into the net by City full-back Jack Walker. Just before the end of the game, Pat Finnerhan completed the scoring, although his shot took a deflection off Heath. The final result was one of several that saw City improve their form in the second half of the season and the Blues eventually ended the season in a respectable ninth place. *NB Many statistical records give one of Rowan's goals to Finnerhan.*

Manchester City: Williams, Walker, Robson, Nash, Bowman, McBride, Meredith, Finnerhan, Rowan, McReddie, Milarvie

Lincoln City: Roberts, McFarlane, Heath, Britain, Mettam, Osborne, Smallman, Duckworth, Lees, Blewitt, Frettingham

Season: 1894/95

P	W	D	L	F	A	PTS
30	14	3	13	82	72	31

Division: Two
Position: Ninth
Manager: Joshua Parlby
Top Goalscorer: Pat Finnerhan (15)
Average Attendance: 6,000

Billy Meredith signed from Chirk and spent two periods with City: 1894-1906 and 1921-1924. In total, he played 501 games, scoring 158 goals.

Manchester City v. Darwen

18 February 1899

Football League Second Division
Hyde Road, Manchester
Attendance: 8,000

Manchester City 10   Darwen 0
F Williams (5)
Meredith (3)
Dougal, S. Smith

Automatic promotion and relegation were introduced in this season, and City were keen to grasp the opportunity to move out of the Second Division. They started the season in fine style, defeating Grimsby Town 7-2; in fact, goalscoring was something that City seemed particularly good at, as only two games in the season ended without the Blues scoring. The highlight of the season must have been the thrashing handed out to Darwen for the biggest win of the campaign.

Darwen were given very little chance of beating the free-scoring Blues. They were stuck at the bottom of the League, having only scored 12 goals and conceded 78 in twenty games. City soon took the lead through Fred Williams, and then added two further goals before the half-time interval. George Dougal headed a second from a Billy Gillespie cross and then Billy Meredith netted to give City a comfortable lead. On the resumption of play in the second half, City continued to attack and Doc Holmes found Meredith, who charged along the wing and then passed to F. Williams, who with a high shot, scored his second goal of the game.

City continued the pressure and Meredith had a goal disallowed after the referee consulted his linesman. F. Williams then found the net with a particularly fine effort, which flew past several Darwen players. City now had a lead of five goals, but it soon became six when Dougal sent in a cross to Meredith and he finished in style. F. Williams added a seventh, following good work by his striking partner, Dougal. The next goal came about following one of Darwen's occasional visits into the City penalty area. Dick Ray, however, broke the move down and passed the ball back to 'keeper Charlie Williams, who kicked the ball upfield to F. Williams, who duly placed the ball out of the reach of Whittaker. F. Williams created an individual record for the afternoon by scoring five goals, becoming the first player to score that many in a game for City.

The Blues then toyed with Darwen, who were now a totally demoralized team and, when Gillespie and Dougal combined down the wing, William 'Stockport' Smith scored, bringing the total to nine. C. Williams was then tested, when Darwen were awarded a free-kick just outside the area, but he saved well. Immediately afterwards, City launched one final attack. Some quick passing by various City players ended in Meredith taking the City score into double figures.

No further scoring took place as a very one-sided game concluded. At the end of the season, City won promotion to achieve their pre-season aspirations.

Manchester City: C. Williams, Read, Ray, Moffatt, B Smith, Holmes, Meredith, S Smith, Gillespie, F. Williams, Dougal

Darwen: Whittaker, Woolfall, Ratcliffe, Sinclair, Dyson, Pilkington, Wilson, Livesey, Rutherford, Bleasdale, McIvor

The view of *Athletic News* on the game was, 'After such a victorious issue, you would expect to hear of clockwork movements from wing to wing and all the rest of the Aston cum Stokey, Villa class jargon, such was far from being the case, Gillespie's, Dougal's and Meredith's goals were superb individual efforts.'

Season: 1898/99

P	W	D	L	F	A	PTS
34	23	6	5	92	35	52

Division: Two
Position: First
Manager: Sam Ormerod
Top Goalscorer: Billy Meredith (30)
Average Attendance: 10,000

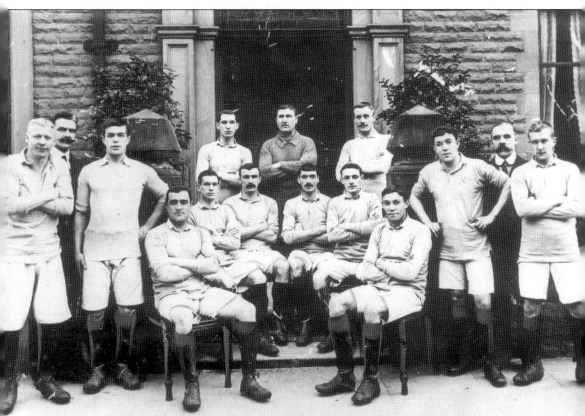

This photograph shows Manchester City at the beginning of the twentieth century in front of the Grand Hotel.

MANCHESTER CITY V. DERBY COUNTY

9 September 1899

Football League First Division
Hyde Road, Manchester
Attendance: 22,000

Manchester City 4	Derby County 0

Meredith (2)
Gillespie, Ross

With only two defeats in the second half of the 1898/99 season, City swept to the top of the League, winning the championship by six points. This meant that the dawning of a new century was to bring First Division football to Ardwick for the first time. Initially, there were concerns as to whether or not Hyde Road would be capable of holding the potentially larger crowds. However, with the help of Chester's-Thompson, who were one of the biggest benefactors at City, and a local brewing family, improvements were made to the ground – including the building of a new stand, which increased the capacity to 28,000, and the painting of pitch-side perimeters in club colours. A new-look Hyde Road stadium was therefore set for the visit of Derby County, FA Cup finalists the previous year, in Manchester City's first home game in the top flight of English football.

The season had begun the previous Saturday, when the Blues missed out in a seven-goal thriller at Blackburn Rovers, Meredith, Ross and F. Williams having scored City's first ever goals at the highest level.

The side were determined to put on a good performance, and the crowd were not to be

Left: Jimmy Ross signed from Burnley and played 70 games for City between 1897-1902, scoring 22 goals. Right: Billy Gillespie signed from Lincoln City and played 231 games between 1897-1905, scoring 132 goals.

disappointed. From the start, City attacked and Derby's goalkeeper, Fryer, had to make magnificent saves to deny the rampant Blues a much-deserved opening goal. The fervent supporters' patience was rewarded on the half-hour mark when Fred Williams centred towards Billy Gillespie. The big centre forward won the ball in typical style, following a goalmouth scramble, and pushed it over the line, inside the near post, to claim a hotly-disputed goal. Before half-time, veteran Jimmy Ross added a second, with a fine low shot.

The pattern of play in the second half followed that of the first, as City continued to dominate proceedings. Derby's defenders were having their work cut out in trying to deal with the attacks from City's right wing, and it was no surprise when Billy Meredith scored a third goal.

The fourth was a vintage goal from Meredith, which is best described in his own words: 'A free kick had been given against us, and I was quite near my own goal when I fastened onto the ball, carrying it at my toes I galloped down the field with the whole Derby team hot on my heels. Keeping the lead the whole length of the field, I found myself with only Fryer to beat. Giving a mighty kick, I let fly at the goal and the 'keeper only just managed to touch the ball before it curled itself into the corner of the net. I rather like that goal, thinking it above average.'

The majority of the crowd also liked it, and thought it a superb effort. It showed the whole of the First Division that City were there to stay and stay they did, finishing seventh, one place below Derby County.

Manchester City: C. Williams, Read, Jones, Moffatt, Smith, Holmes, Meredith, Ross, Gillespie, F. Williams, Dougal

Derby County: Fryer, Methven, Staley, Cox, Paterson, May, Bradbury, Bloomer, Crump, Wombwell, McQueen

Referee: T Armitt (Leek)

Billy Meredith commented in the *Topical Times* some years after the game, 'From the corner flag, I kicked at goal and the ball curled under the bar, but striking the upright bounced back. To save disputes, Gillespie promptly headed it into the net, but it was agreed that I had scored the goal alright and, at that time, I was supposed to have taken out a patent for goals of that kind'.

Season: 1899/1900

P	W	D	L	F	A	PTS
34	13	8	13	50	44	34

Division: One
Position: Seventh
Manager: Sam Ormerod
Top Goalscorer: Billy Meredith (14)
Average Attendance: 16,000

Barnsley v. Manchester City

14 April 1903

Football League Second Division
Oakwell, Barnsley
Attendance: 5,000

Barnsley 0   Manchester City 3
                   Meredith
                   Bannister
                   Gillespie

Following relegation the previous season, City were determined to bounce back at the first attempt – and what a successful attempt it was for the Blues. They won 25 of their 34 league games and scored 95 goals. In an amazing run from January, City won six consecutive matches, scoring 35 goals and conceding 3. With the team riding high at the top of the table, they achieved unbelievable results. At Hyde Road, they beat Burnley (6-0), Burslem Port Vale (7-1), Small Heath (4-0) and Gainsborough Trinity (7-1), and on their travels, Burton United (5-0).

Victory in the final game of the season would mean that City would be promoted to the First Division as champions. The Blues went into the game at Barnsley missing four key players: Doc Holmes, Sammy Frost, Tom Hynds and Fred Threlfall. It was, therefore, not particularly surprising that the men from Yorkshire dominated the opening stages of the game, believing they had strong appeals for a penalty, when Alec Hellewell felt he had been fouled when through on goal, but all protests were disregarded by the referee.

Left: *Jack Hillman signed from Burnley and played 124 games for City between 1902-1906.*
Right: *Sandy Turnbull signed from Hurlford Thistle and played 119 games between 1902-1906, scoring 60 goals.*

Barnsley's next attack saw Green put over a cross that Underwood failed to meet with his head. Luck was on City's side, when Peter Slater mis-kicked a clearance, but Johnny McMahon was alert to avert any danger. City gradually began to impose their authority on the match, and it was no surprise when Billy Gillespie opened the scoring for the champions-elect with an easy chance. Jimmy Bannister then further increased the lead with a beautiful shot, which gave Greaves in the Barnsley goal little chance of saving. So in command were City, that even when Gillespie missed an open goal before the interval, there was no undue worry, such was the Blues' dominance.

City continued to attack the Barnsley goal on the resumption of the second half. Greaves saved well from Dearden, and then Frank Booth had an opportunity to further increase City's lead, but put his shot directly into the hands of the Barnsley 'keeper. Barnsley were unlucky to see a goal disallowed by the referee, when Underwood had finished off a fine shot from Hellewell. It was not destined to be Barnsley's game: Jack Hillman saved a Lees penalty and, minutes before the end, Billy Meredith secured the points for City, easily converting a pass from Booth.

With the right results, tactical direction and financial investment, City were promoted into the First Division. The promotion-winning team was to form the basis for one of the most eventful periods in City's history.

Barnsley: Greaves, Hay, McCartney, Bennett, Lees, Oxspring, Alec Hellewell, Green, A. Hellewell, Underwood, Mawson

Manchester City: Hillman, McMahon, Slater, Bevan, Dearden, McOustra, Meredith, Bannister, Gillespie, Turnbull, Booth

Season: 1902/03

P	W	D	L	F	A	PTS
34	25	4	5	95	29	54

Division:	Two
Position:	First
Manager:	Tom Maley
Top Goalscorer:	Billy Gillespie (30)
Average Attendance:	16,000

MANCHESTER CITY V. BOLTON WANDERERS.

23 April 1904

FA Cup final
Crystal Palace, London
Attendance: 61,374

Manchester City 1   Bolton Wanderers 0
Meredith

City's record in the cup had been negligible, never having advanced beyond the second round. Now they were on the threshold of taking one of football's major prizes. In the week before the final, preparations had been feverish. On the day of the game, all pubs in the Ardwick area closed down for the day, and everybody travelled en masse to London.

Bolton were a Second Division side with no prominent players, although they were a hardworking, strong team. City, on the other hand, were untouchable in every department.

With the approach of the Cup Final, Billy Meredith's national fame came to prominence. Railway posters advertising excursions to the game portrayed Meredith scoring the winning goal, in a similar fashion to the way in which the match actually would be won.

On the day of the final, the crowd was by far the largest City had played in front of, but the authorities at Crystal Palace were disappointed, as it was below the expected crowd size for a final, the main requirement being for fans to travel from the north. It was the first time two Lancashire clubs had competed in the Cup Final, and both sets of supporters were warmed up by the St Joseph's Industrial school band, while outside the ground was a fun-fair. A revolutionary new idea for covering games was being tried out by reporters of *The Athletic News* in 'Balloonatic' – a gas-filled balloon that was being piloted by Percival Spencer, a famous aeronaut.

Meredith led the City team out, calmly chewing on his trademark toothpick. He won the toss, and chose to attack the goal where the City supporters were massed. There was little to choose between both sides in the opening exchanges. Then, on twenty minutes, George Livingstone made a pass out to the right for Meredith, who forged ahead, ghosted past the Bolton defence with practically no opposition, and fired passed the goalkeeper, Davies. One fan was so elated at seeing the goal, he attempted to invade the pitch to congratulate the scorer, only to be led away by five policemen. Bolton were emphatic that the goal was offside and, for years afterwards, their supporters claimed they had been robbed.

City continued to dominate and, when the interval arrived, they were certainly entitled to their one-goal lead. The second half was similar to the first, in that neither side seemed able to establish consistency in their play. Billy Gillespie and Sandy Turnbull both failed to convert good chances and, although Bolton pressed hard, their possession rarely troubled City, who had the game well within their control.

As the final whistle blew, the players raced for the enclosure, as the crowds swarmed across the pitch to where the trophy was to be presented. Colonial secretary Lord Alfred Lyttlelton, alongside the Prime Minister at the time A.J. Balfour, a former patron of City, presented the FA Cup to Meredith.

There were eleven heroes for City that day, and the fans would remember them all. City were very proud of their victory and enjoyed themselves immensely. Everybody would remember the game's winning goal that had been depicted on all those railway posters advertising excursions to the game.

Manchester City: Hillman, McMahon, Burgess, Frost, Hynds, Ashworth, Meredith, Livingstone, Gillespie, Turnbull, Booth

Bolton Wanderers: Davies, Brown, Struthers, Clifford, Greenhalgh, Freebairn, Stokes, Marsh, Yenson, White, Taylor

Referee. A.J. Barker (Hanley)

Billy Meredith, when asked of his side's chances, said 'Good, we ought to win, you never know but if we play anything like our normal game, the Cup is ours. All the boys are going for all they are worth. If today's game had been a League match, it would have been a pretty certain couple of points, but this is the Cup Final and, well, anything might happen.'

The *Manchester Evening Chronicle*, on Monday 25 April, commented on the solitary goal: 'The validity of the only goal of the match, which was secured by William Meredith, has been seriously questioned by Boltonians, but expert judges avow that Meredith's position was a correct one when he received the ball from Livingstone and, after rounding Struthers, shot into the net. There is no doubt, however, that on several occasions the speedy Welshman was in an off-side position, but on the momentous occasion under notice, it did not appear so, and, what is to the point, Mr Barker, the referee, was of the opinion not.

It was indeed appropriate that City's captain should score the goal that brought the FA Cup to Manchester. He is the oldest playing member of the club, its most brilliant exponent, and, without a doubt, the best outside right in the kingdom. This is no mere gush because of the trend of events on Saturday, but an acknowledged fact throughout the land. On Saturday, Freebairn was crossed over to hold him in hand, but he failed to do so, while Struthers, the left-back, will remember the wily Willie for many a long day. The scoring of the goal was a case of one cunning Taffy outwitting another, though Davies could not at all be blamed for not securing the ball.

It is rather singular that the all-important goal was the only one, which Meredith secured in the competition of the City's 12 goals.

In connection with the match, one unique record should be mentioned. On 16 April, the Celtic club, of which Mr Willie Maley is secretary, won the Scottish Cup, and on 23 April, his brother Tom's team carried off the English Cup.'

Season: 1903/04

P	W	D	L	F	A	PTS
34	19	6	9	71	45	44

Division:	One
Position:	Second
Manager:	Tom Maley
Top Goalscorer:	Sandy Turnbull (22)
Average Attendance:	20,000

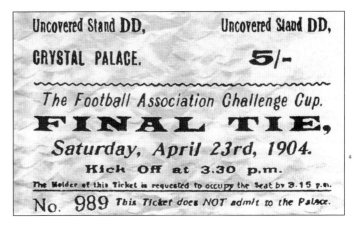

A 1904 FA Cup final ticket.

MANCHESTER CITY V. WOOLWICH ARSENAL

1 September 1906

League First Division
Hyde Road, Manchester
Attendance: 18,000

Manchester City 1   Woolwich Arsenal 4
Dorsett   *Kyle (2)*
                           Coleman, Satterthwaite

The most remarkable feature of the opening fixture of the season at Hyde Road, was the effect of the intense heat upon the City players, in contrast to the comparative immunity of the Arsenal players. This was a match not likely to be forgotten by those who took part in it, as well as the thousands who watched it – the temperature thermometer registered something like 90 degrees in the shade.

City started the game at a great disadvantage, fielding virtually a new team, following the mass suspension of players for the scandal that flared up the previous season, following illegal payments and bribery allegations.

Woolwich dominated the opening exchanges and, had they been able to utilize their chances and shoot accurately, they might have taken the lead long before they did. As it was, the game had been in progress for over half an hour before they scored their opening goal. Kyle made the best of a fine centre from Neave and shot hard into the net. Within a couple of minutes of the opening goal, City lost Irvine Thornley who had left the field very ill through sunstroke and

Manchester City FC, 1906/07. From left to right, back row: Baldwin, Smith, Buchan, Norgrove, Eadie, Steele, Davies, Hill, Kelso, Evans, Taylor. Front row: Whittaker, Hamblett, Grieve, Christie, Conlin, Young, Banks, Stewart. Seated: Thornley, Fisher, Dorsett. This squad was put together by Harry Newbould in the aftermath of Maley's departure. After avoiding relegation, they finished third the following term, but any hopes of another title challenge soon faded twelve months later when the team dropped into the Second Division.

took no further part in the game.

Six minutes before the interval, Coleman scored a second for Arsenal. City then lost Jimmy Conlin, who had been playing with a handkerchief over his head to protect himself from the scorching rays of the sun and, although there were others showing signs of distress, City managed to finish the first half with nine men on the field.

The extent of their suffering was revealed after the interval. When only eight men reappeared, the centre forward Robert Grieve being unable to turn out, City changed their formation for the second half to three forwards; three half backs, a full back and a goalkeeper. They were at a great disadvantage, but managed to keep the Woolwich players at bay for some time. Conlin returned, but the Blues troubles were not over yet, for, after George Dorsett had pulled a goal back for City, he collapsed under the strain off the heat and City were back down to eight men.

Arsenal then scored a further two goals, one through Satterthwaite and a second from Kyle, and City lost a fourth player, Tom Kelso. The City players were falling like pins, and the loss of Jimmy Buchan meant the thin Blue line had to hold out in the unbearable heat with six players, until the final whistle blew.

It was a great baptism of fire for new secretary/manager Harry Newbold, especially when his team conceded nine goals in their next fixture at Everton. City were the one team in the country to collapse under the great heat, and one could not help but sympathise with them for the cruel misfortune they had suffered.

Manchester City: Davies, Christie, Kelso, Steele, Buchan, Dorsett, Stewart, Thornley, Grieve, Jones, Conlin

Woolwich Arsenal: Ashcroft, Cross, Sharp, Bigden, Sands, McEachrane, Garbutt, Coleman, Kyle, Satterthwaite, Neave

Referee: A.J. Barker (Hanley)

Season: 1906/07

P	W	D	L	F	A	PTS
38	10	12	16	53	77	32

Division:	One
Position:	Seventeenth
Manager:	Harry Newbould
Top Goalscorer:	Irvine Thornley (14)
Average Attendance:	22,000

EVERTON V. MANCHESTER CITY

3 September 1906

Football League First Division
Goodison Park
Attendance: 16,000

Everton 9	Manchester City 1
Young (4)	*Fisher*
Abbott (2), Settle (2)	
Taylor	

The first task City had to perform before the season started was to find a new manager: Harry Newbould accepted the job. He then had the task of finding players who were good enough to represent City. It was clearly going to be a long hard season and, in the second game of the campaign, they suffered their heaviest defeat in a match ever, a record that still stands to this day.

As can be gathered from the scoreline, this was a very one-sided game and Everton were far superior to City. Everton commenced the match very brightly and Taylor scored from a corner, after Frank Davies had cleared. Following this, Jimmy Buchan almost equalized for City when he worked the ball into a favourable position, but his final shot did not trouble the Everton 'keeper, Scott. Everton then attacked, and Settle added two goals in rapid succession. From this point on, Everton simply had matters their own way. Davies did not create a feeling of security with his clearances, and a defence that was greatly harassed did not help him, allowing Abbott to register a fourth goal with a tremendous drive. Five minutes from the half-time interval, Young chested home a fifth goal. Young was a chief source of danger on the left wing, baffling City's half-backs and, when Sharp raced away, Young scored two further goals, Everton's sixth and seventh of the game.

Left: *Jimmy Buchan signed for City from Woolwich Arsenal and played 164 games between 1905-1911, scoring 10 goals.* Right: *George Dorsett signed for City from WBA and played in 211 games between 1901-1912, scoring 65 goals.*

The response from City was minimal, although George Dorsett was prominent and he saw a brilliant shot skim the bar. The defence of Everton, the current Cup holders, was then breached, in one of the occasional attacks on goal from City. George Stewart broke away and centred to Jimmy Conlin, whose shot crashed against the upright, but debutant signing James Fisher from Brighton & Hove Albion netted.

Everton were always dangerous, and Davies was frequently called upon, but he was beaten on two further occasions near the finish when Abbott, and then Young, with his fourth goal of the game, completed the rout.

City were comprehensively beaten and their defence had performed half-heartedly. The whole team were out-classed against a side which was too powerful for them, and the goals came with a rapidity seldom witnessed in the League.

Everton: Scott, W Balmer, Crelly, Booth, Taylor, Abbott, Sharp, Bolton, Young, Settle, G. Wilson

Manchester City: Davies, Christie, Norgrove, Steele, Buchan, Dorsett, Stewart, Fisher, Grieve, Jones, Conlin

Referee: F. Kirkham (Preston)

Jimmy Conlin signed for City from Bradford City and played in 175 games between 1904-1911 scoring 30 goals.

29

MANCHESTER CITY V. LEEDS CITY

23 April 1910

Football League Second Division
Hyde Road, Manchester
Attendance: 16,000

Manchester City 3   Leeds City 0
Dorsett, Wynn, Conlin

Manchester City entered the 1909/10 season looking to bring some stability and success to the club. In order to achieve these aims, they had to gain promotion. As March approached, Blues supporters started to believe that this could be their year for the Second Division title. Despite suffering defeat in 'four-pointer' games against Derby County and Oldham Athletic, the Championship was won against Leeds City.

The Leeds captain won the toss and decided to protect his team from the wind, which was so strong that it would handicap a team having to battle against it. However, City soon put their supporters' minds at rest, when they scored twice in the space of nine minutes. Jimmy Conlin fired home a fine drive, and George Wynn scored with a left-foot shot from some twenty yards, beating Bromage in the Leeds goal.

Despite the advantage of the wind, Leeds were making a very disappointing show. The forwards, in particular, were highly ineffective, and Jack Lyall in the City goal had very little to

Left: *Jack Lyall signed for City from Sheffield Wednesday and played in 44 games between 1909-1911.* Right: *Billy 'Lot' Jones signed for City from Rushton Druids and played in 339 games between 1903-1919, scoring 80 goals.*

do throughout the afternoon. The men from Yorkshire were no match for a City side who were speedier, trickier and played with a better understanding. The Blues continued to apply pressure: Billy Lot Jones was through on goal, when he was tripped up near the penalty box, but the free-kick brought no reward. However, three minutes from the interval, George Dorsett scored City's third goal of the game, shooting past Bromage from a free-kick outside the box.

It was at this point that Leeds had their best chance: Roberts showed a fine turn of speed, and finished with a shot that grazed the crossbar. So, with three goals to their account and the wind in their favour, many City supporters looked forward to the prospect of City giving their goal average a boost. Lot Jones had a shot smothered but, apart from that, little of note was seen from either side, as the game degenerated into little more than a scramble. The finishing power of both sides continued to be lacking in effectiveness. The crowd encouraged City to attack and Bromage produced the save of the game to deny Tom Holford scoring a fourth for the Blues.

Tom Kelso signed for City from Third Lanark and played in 151 games between 1906-1913, scoring 3 goals.

The final game of the season saw City beaten 3-2 at Wolverhampton, but it hardly mattered, as over the course of the previous weeks, their nearest promotion rivals wilted under the pressure, allowing City to finish the season as champions.

Manchester City: Lyall, Kelso, Jackson, Thornley, Wilkinson, Dorsett, Gould, Wynn, Holford, Jones, Conlin

Leeds City: Bromage, White, Affleck, Horsley, Morris, Cubberley, Roberts, Mulholland, McLeod, Ackerley, Croot

Season: 1909/10

P	W	D	L	F	A	PTS
38	23	8	7	81	40	54

Division:	Two
Position:	First
Manager:	Harry Newbould
Top Goalscorer:	George Dorsett/Billy Lot Jones (14)
Average Attendance:	18,000

MANCHESTER CITY V. PRESTON NORTH END

20 April 1921

Football League First Division
Hyde Road, Manchester
Attendance: 20,000

Manchester City 5	Preston North End 1
Browell (3)	*Roberts*
Barnes (2)	

Back in the early 1920s, City embarked on a run of 34 consecutive home games without a loss. In fact, they only lost one game, against Birmingham City on 9 September 1922, in their final two seasons before leaving Hyde Road. The penultimate season saw City ending the 1920/21 season with a seven-match unbeaten run, and one of the games to feature in that period was against Preston North End.

Both teams introduced players for their League debuts, City's latest acquisition being Jack Warner from the Customhouse Club of London. Preston started the game brightly, and both their wing forwards were prominent in attack, but their finishing was not so strong. Croft was guilty of missing a splendid chance, and Roberts forced Jim Goodchild to make a great save.

Eventually, City forced themselves into the game and, after twenty minutes, Horace Barnes opened the scoring with a wonderful shot into the far corner of the net. Preston, however, continued to trouble the City defence, but a combination of poor finishing by Croft and a fine save by Goodchild from Roberts left City going in at the interval with a one-goal lead.

Left: *Horace Barnes signed for City from Derby County and played in 308 games between 1914-1924 scoring 198 goals.* Right: *Tommy Browell signed for City from Everton and played in 208 games between 1913-1926 scoring 157 goals.*

Preston were again the more assertive at the start of the second half, but a dashing effort by Tommy Browell and a storming shot from Barnes provided the prelude to a period of aggressiveness by City. When Warner found Browell in a good position, the centre forward hooked the ball over two defenders and ran in to score a magnificent goal. Five minutes later, Browell scored again, when quick movement by the former Everton player found him with only Causer to beat in goal. City's lead was further increased with a penalty kick from Browell, given for an earlier handball infringement by Doolan. The last three goals had been scored in the short space of eleven minutes.

Roberts pulled a goal back for Preston ten minutes from time with a shot that seemed to strike the inside of the post and rebound into the net. On eighty-two minutes, City scored again. The referee turned down strong appeals for a penalty and, as Causer cleared the ball, Barnes charged it down and it rebounded into an empty net.

Victory ensured City finished as runners-up to Burnley in the League, and Tommy Browell finished as top goalscorer for the season with 31 goals.

Jim Goodchild signed for City from Southampton common and played in 347 games between 1911-1927.

Manchester City: Goodchild, Cookson, Allan, Fayers, Woosnam, Hamill, Broad, Warner, Browell, Barnes, Murphy

Preston North End: Causer, Hamilton, Doolan, Waddell, McCall, Mercer, Rawlings, Jefferis, Roberts, Woodhouse, Croft

Referee: H. Ward (Kirkham)

Season: 1920/21

P	W	D	L	F	A	PTS
42	24	6	12	70	50	54

Division:	One
Position:	Second
Manager:	Ernest Mangnall
Top Goalscorer:	Tommy Browell (31)
Average Attendance:	31,000

MANCHESTER CITY V. SHEFFIELD UNITED

25 August 1923

Football League First Division
Maine Road, Manchester
Attendance: 58,159

Manchester City 2   Sheffield United 1
Barnes   *Johnson*
Johnson

This game has to go down as probably one of the most memorable in the history of Manchester City. It was the first game to be played at their spectacular new Maine Road Stadium in Moss Side.

The stadium was designed to hold 80,000 people and it only took five months to build. One stand was seated and covered and the others were tiers of terracing, for many of the loyal followers from the Hyde Road days plus numerous others who were curious to have a look at the new stadium. This was a point not lost on the local newspapers at the time, which tended to focus their labours more on the construction of the stadium than the action that took place on the pitch.

Max Woosnam, captain for the day, led the City players on to the field of play. The Lord Mayor of Manchester, Councillor Cundiffe, opened events by being introduced to the players and then carrying out an official kick-off. Although in accordance with Football League rules, the ball was actually returned to the centre for City's Tom Johnson to commence the game properly.

Maine Road, taken shortly after City moved there in 1923.

City welcomed back two star players, Eli Fletcher and Sam Cookson. They also included new signing, Alec Donaldson, a winger from Bolton Wanderers.

The first half ended in stalemate, although Johnson and Horace Barnes forced the Sheffield 'keeper, Gough, to make two fine saves.

The second half saw City increase the pressure and, after sixty-eight minutes, inside forward Barnes had the honour of scoring the first goal at Maine Road, when he breached the defence after accepting a cross from Donaldson to fire home, much to the delight of the partisan crowd. Three minutes later, the City faithful were in raptures when Johnson increased City's lead, after Gough had saved his initial attempt.

Shortly afterwards, the Blues had a chance to increase their lead further, but Frank Roberts claimed his little bit of City history when he became the first player to miss a penalty at Maine Road, shooting straight at the goalkeeper.

With just two minutes to play Sheffield United, down to ten men, pulled a goal back with a header from centre forward Harry Johnson, which found its way past Jim Mitchell in the City net.

The Blues hung on to win the game and a new epoch in the club's history had begun.

Manchester City: Mitchell, Cookson, Fletcher, Hamill, Woosnam, Pringle, Donaldson, Roberts, Johnson, Barnes, Murphy

Sheffield United: Gough, Cook, Milton, Pantling, Waugh, Green, Mercer, Sampy, Johnson, Gillespie, Tunstal

Referee: J. Rowcroft (Bolton)

Season: 1923/24

P	W	D	L	F	A	PTS
42	15	12	15	54	71	42

Division:	One
Position:	Eleventh
Manager:	Ernest Mangnall
Top Goalscorer:	Horace Barnes (22)
Average Attendance:	27,000

MANCHESTER CITY V. BURNLEY

24 October 1925

Football League First Division
Maine Road, Manchester
Attendance: 19,740

Manchester City 8
Browell (5)
Roberts, Johnson, Hicks

Burnley 3
Hill, Kelly, Page

This season was expected to see City return to the top of the table and challenge for the game's major honours. The season, however, developed into one of inconsistency. The Blues were becoming totally unpredictable, with fine performances one week and abysmal ones the next. The FA Cup saw them reach the final, with handsome victories against Crystal Palace (11-4) and Clapton Orient (6-0). The League saw convincing triumphs over Manchester United (6-1) and Leicester City (5-1), but embarrassing defeats at Bury (5-6), Huddersfield Town (1-5) and Sunderland (3-5). The inconsistency was such that, in one week, they were humiliated by Sheffield United (3-8), having achieved an incredible 8-3 victory against Burnley a few days earlier.

Burnley's experiences at Maine Road had not been very memorable and they had never beaten City, so the trouncing they received in this remarkable game was as bad as they had ever fared at this ground. Tommy Browell opened the scoring for City, but that was soon

Left: *Tommy Johnson signed for City from Dalton and played 359 games between 1919-1930 scoring 170 goals.* Right: *Sam Cookson signed for City from Macclesfield Town and played 306 games between 1918-1928 scoring 1 goal.*

cancelled out by a goal from Hill. Browell then got his second of the game, just before half-time and, although City only had a narrow lead at the half-time interval, they were very much superior and had reduced Burnley to a very poor side.

Browell added a further two goals for City directly after the interval. George Hicks immediately followed with a fifth, and Tommy Johnson added a sixth from the penalty spot. Burnley then pulled back two goals in as many minutes, through Kelly and Page, and, for a time, looked very much like further reducing the arrears.

There was more method and pace in the way City played, and their forwards were too quick for the Burnley defence and came back with two further goals in the final few minutes of the game, Browell and Roberts increasing the lead to eight. Browell had now scored five goals in a veritable day of joy for him and his colleagues. The joy was not to last at the end of the season though, because City's failure to gain a point from their final game of the season against Newcastle United saw them relegated to the Second Division.

Manchester City: Mitchell, Cookson, McCloy, Coupland, Cowan, Pringle, Bradford, Roberts, Browell, Johnson, Hicks

Burnley: Dawson, McCluggage, Waterfield, Hill, Armitage, Parkin, Bruton, Kelly, Beal, Cross, Page

Season: 1925/26

P	W	D	L	F	A	PTS
42	12	11	19	89	100	35

Division:	One
Position:	Twenty-first
Manager:	David Ashworth
Top Goalscorer:	Frank Roberts (30)
Average Attendance:	32,000

MANCHESTER CITY V. CRYSTAL PALACE

20 February 1926

FA Cup Fifth Round
Maine Road, Manchester
Attendance: 51,630

Manchester City 11
Roberts (5)
Browell (3)
Johnson, Austin, Hicks

Crystal Palace 4
Cherrett (2)
Clarke, McCracken

One of the most remarkable games in which Manchester City have ever participated, was their meeting with Crystal Palace in a Cup tie at Maine Road. It was a game made extraordinary by virtue of the transformation that took place in the second half. Until the interval, there was absolutely no comparison between the teams, as City thoroughly outclassed Palace with a glut of goals.

After four minutes, McCracken fouled George Hicks and Billy Austin scored with a penalty, after which, the goals began to fly in. Frank Roberts then scored in the twelfth and twenty-second minutes, Tommy Johnson in the twenty-fifth minute, and Roberts completed his hat-trick on thirty minutes. When Tommy Browell added a further two goals in the last few minutes of the first half, City had practically done as they liked against helpless opposition. The margin at the interval would have been greater, but for some splendid goal-keeping by Callender.

It was perhaps only natural that, with such an advantage, City would ease up in the second half, but this nearly cost them dearly. Palace seized the opportunity of pulling themselves together, and they took advantage of City's complacency. Against all belief, they fought back in great style. Cherrett scored a fine goal in the fifty-fifth minute, but City always had the game well in hand, as shown by the fact that whenever Palace scored, City promptly replied with another. Browell made it 8-1 after fifty-eight minutes, but Cherrett immediately pulled one back with his second goal of the game and, following two wonderful saves by Callender from Austin and Roberts, Palace scored two further quick goals. Clarke scored from a penalty after the first shot had been parried by Jim Goodchild, and then McCracken put away another chance.

The City defence was now under severe pressure and the crowd were full of praise for the fighting qualities of the Crystal Palace players, some for a short time entertaining brief hopes of a replay. City were mainly indebted to their forwards for their victory, and Roberts took full advantage of some disorganized defensive tactics and added two more goals in the seventy-fifth and eighty-second minutes. Just before the end, Hicks had the satisfaction of scoring City's eleventh goal, finally ending any thoughts of a remarkable Palace comeback.

The goal-keeping of Callender was one of the features of the match and, at the conclusion, he was carried shoulder-high by enthusiastic spectators.

It was an odd season for City: they made history with the thrashing of Palace, lost the FA Cup Final to Bolton, and, to make matters worse, were relegated.

Manchester City: Goodchild, Cookson, McCloy, Coupland, Cowan, Pringle, Austin, Browell, Roberts, Johnson, Hicks

Crystal Palace: Callender, Little, Cross, McCracken, Coyle, Greener, Harry, Blakemore, Cherrett, Hawkes, Clarke

A cartoon of Charlie Pringle. Pringle signed for City from St Mirren and played 216 games between 1922-28, scoring 1 goal.

Manchester City v. Bolton Wanderers

24 April 1926

FA Cup final
Wembley Stadium, London
Attendance: 91,547

Manchester City 0   Bolton Wanderers 1
                         Jack

It was reported in many newspapers after this game, that there would be small chance of another FA Cup Final being played at Wembley Stadium, and that both Lancashire clubs would hold the honour of playing in the last ever final.

The reason for all this speculation was because, for nearly an hour, all approaches to Wembley were congested with people, who had started arriving at 3 a.m. in order to purchase tickets for the final. Ticket chaos caused many angry confrontations between supporters and ticket touts, who had marked up the value of tickets quite significantly.

Bolton started as favourites, mainly because City were languishing in the lower regions of the First Division. Bolton dominated the first fifteen minutes of the game, as the Blues appeared a little overwhelmed by the occasion. They were overrun during this first period and Wanderers wasted three good chances, in particular David Jack, to gain the lead.

City gradually began to get into the game, and the speed of their moves led to a couple of chances going their way. There was very little difference between the teams, and the game remained goal-less at half time. In the second half, Bolton 'keeper Dick Pym made a couple of fine saves, as City fought desperately to find an opening goal. He saved on his knees from Frank Roberts and, just as Bolton were beginning to fight back, Pym produced a match-winning save from a header by Tommy Browell.

It seemed now that one goal would settle the game and, with twelve minutes remaining, the game swung Bolton's way. A flowing move from Wanderers saw the ball go out to Vizard, who

rescued it near the corner flag and centred to Jack, who was stood unmarked in the centre of the box. He lunged with his left foot to send the ball into the net for the only goal of the game. The final few minutes saw plenty of further action, as the Blues tried to force an equalizer, but it was not to be.

The result was a fair one, although everybody associated with the Blues found it difficult to accept. After the Final, City had to pick themselves up and turn their attention back to fighting for their position in the League. City's failure to gain a point from their final game of the season against Newcastle United sent them into the Second Division.

City's skipper is introduced to King George V prior to the Cup Final with Bolton Wanderers.

Manchester City: Goodchild, Cookson, McCloy, Pringle, Cowan, McMullan, Austin, Browell, Roberts, Johnson, Hicks

Bolton Wanderers: Pym, Haworth, Greenhalgh, Nuttall, Seddon, Jennings, Butler, Jack, JR Smith, J Smith, Vizard

Referee: J. Baker (Crewe)

City's man of the match was McMullan, and this is what the *Daily Mail* had to say about him: 'McMullan was the greatest-hearted man of twenty-two. He was half-back, full-back and forward, all combined in one. His attack was as good as his defence, and it was certainly not his fault that his team were beaten.'

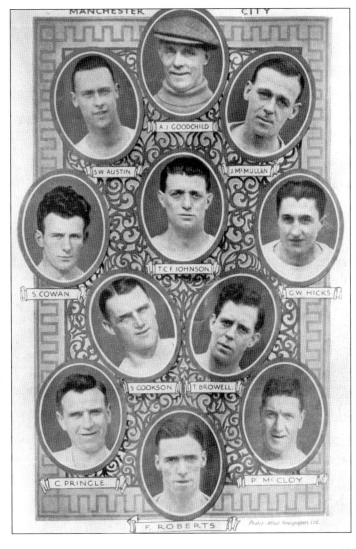

City's FA Cup final team.

MANCHESTER CITY V. BRADFORD CITY

7 May 1927

Football League Second Division
Maine Road, Manchester
Attendance: 50,000

Manchester City 8   Bradford City 0
Johnson (3)
Broadhurst (2)
Bell, Hicks, Roberts

A huge crowd was present at Maine Road for this encounter, on a very hot day. The atmosphere was electric, as City tried to clinch promotion to the First Division. There was never any doubt that they would not win, but could they score more goals then their nearest rivals, Portsmouth, to gain automatic promotion?

Within six minutes of the start of the game, City were one goal up, when Boot, in the Bradford goal, failed to hold on to a ball that had been swung into the box by Peter Bell. Ten minutes later, Tommy Johnson had increased the lead.

Two goals in the first sixteen minutes was a glorious start, and when the crowd heard that Preston had scored, that gave City an extra incentive. The Blues continued to play football of the highest quality at a blistering pace and, on the half-hour mark, they went further ahead,

Left: *McCloy signed for City from Ayr United and played 157 games between 1925-1932.* Right: *McMullan signed for City from Partick Thistle and played 242 games between 1926-1933, scoring 12 goals.*

with another brilliant goal from George Hicks.

Throughout the second half City were even more dominant, and scored five more, tearing the Bradford defence to ribbons. Seven minutes after the restart, City had scored a fourth goal through a long range shot by Charlie Broadhurst. Minutes later, it was five, when Frank Roberts flicked the ball into the net from Hicks' cross.

The goals continued to come. On sixty-five minutes, Sam Cowan passed to Johnson and he fired home with his left foot. City were then awarded a penalty, after Broadhurst was brought down when through on goal. Johnson converted the penalty to claim his hat-trick.

The crowd were baying for more, and the young centre forward Broadhurst scored an eighth in the last minute. As soon as the final whistle sounded, the crowd surged onto the field of play, eager to congratulate their heroes on getting back into the big time.

It was a further fifteen minutes before the final scoreline from the Portsmouth game was known: they had defeated Preston 5-1. City's goals-per-game average was 1.7705 and Portsmouth's was 1.7755 – the tightest Second Division promotion race ever, had gone against them.

Wonderful and tragic: those are the only words that could describe this season finale at Maine Road, in a game that will never be forgotten. Never had there been such a cruel twist of fate in the history of League football. City had played wonderful football and produced an amazing crop of goals – just one extra goal would have been enough to ensure automatic promotion.

Manchester City: Gray, Cookson, McCloy, Pringle, Cowan, McMullan, Bell, Roberts, Broadhurst, Johnson, Hicks

Bradford City: Boot, Russell, Watson, Knox, Bancroft, Poole, Hamilton, Paterson, Alcock, Batten, McMillan

Referee: T.G. Bryan (Willenhall)

Season: 1926/27

P	W	D	L	F	A	PTS
42	22	10	10	108	61	54

Division:	Two
Position:	Third
Manager:	Peter Hodge
Top Goalscorer:	Tommy Johnson (25)
Average Attendance:	28,000

MANCHESTER CITY V. BURY

30 January 1929

Football League First Division
Maine Road, Manchester
Attendance: 20,000

Manchester City 6	Bury 4
Johnson (2)	*Ball (2)*
Tait, Brook, Tilson, Austin	*Vernon, Bullock*

City had just secured the Second Division championship for the fourth time but, despite the success, they were expected to struggle in the First Division. The Blues, however, surprised many, and continued to win more games than they lost. For goals, they relied largely on Tommy Johnson, who scored with great regularity, including claiming five in a game against Everton at Goodison Park. One game that Johnson featured in was a ten-goal thriller at Maine Road against Lancashire neighbours, Bury.

An unusual feature of the game was that every time Bury scored, City followed suit almost immediately. The visitors opened the scoring when Vernon, the stand-in centre forward, scored on twenty minutes. Tommy Tait then equalized right away for City with a controversial goal: Bury claimed he was offside, but the referee was against them. Eric Brook gave City the lead with a long, high shot, which the Bury 'keeper, Harrison, should have saved, and, before the interval, Billy Austin made it three for the Blues, when he converted a pass from Syd Gibbons.

Ball reduced the lead thirteen minutes into the second half but, as in the first half, City replied promptly when Johnson went through on goal and scored. City had assumed the upper hand in the second half, and Tait was a source of constant trouble to the Bury defenders. Bury pressed forward and, before the end of the game, the great spirit they were showing saw them get close on one or two occasions, with chances falling to Bullock, Amos and Ball.

In the final five minutes, both defences appeared to collapse and four goals were scored. Fred Tilson and Johnson, although they had not been on top form when finishing, scored for City. Bullock and Ball finally found the score sheet for Bury.

City lost just one of their last ten games to finish their first season back in the First Division in eighth place. It had been a successful season and they had achieved their aim of establishing themselves among the elite. Johnson's 38 goals in 39 games created a record for the club that still stands.

Manchester City: Barber, Barrass, McCloy, Gibbons, Cowan, McMullen, Austin, Tilson, Tait, Johnson, Brook

Bury: Harrison, Heap, Adamson, Porter, Finney, Pratt, Gale, Bullock, Vernon, Amos, Ball

Season: 1928/29

P	W	D	L	F	A	PTS
42	18	9	15	95	86	45

Division:	One
Position:	Eighth
Manager:	Peter Hodge
Top Goalscorer:	Tommy Johnson (38)
Average Attendance:	33,000

Eric Brook signed for City from Barnsley and played 501 games between 1928-1940, scoring 180 goals.

OGDEN'S CIGARETTES

E. F. BROOK *(MANCHESTER CITY)*

Manchester City v. Swindon Town

29 January 1930

FA Cup Fourth Round Replay
Maine Road, Manchester
Attendance: 46,082

Manchester City 10   Swindon Town 1
Marshall (5)   *Morris*
Tait (3)
Johnson, Brook

The two teams had met on the Saturday (25 January 1930) and although City had thoroughly overwhelmed the home team, the state of the pitch glued down their forward line and the fixture finished 1-1, with Sam Cowan scoring for City.

The condition of Maine Road for the replay was very different from that at Swindon, and there was only one change to the teams. Webster had to be drafted in to replace the injured Swindon 'keeper, Nash, who had strained his thigh in the first game. With the going good, City were able to show their true brand of football, and Swindon had Webster to thank for the score not being higher than it was.

The game began at an exhilarating pace. City had a succession of raids, but Swindon countered in style and kept the Blues defenders busy for a while, however, they remained unable to get a shot at Fred Barber. Tommy Johnson opened the scoring for City on thirteen minutes, with a left-foot volley which Webster had not even the remotest chance of saving. Bobby Marshall then put City further ahead on twenty-one minutes with a brilliant individual goal. He beat two men to create a shooting chance, and then turned and drove the ball in, well away from Webster.

Left: Ernie Toseland signed for City from Coventry City and played in 413 games between 1929-1939, scoring 75 goals. Right: Matt Barrass signed for City from Sheffield Wednesday and played in172 games between 1926-1933, scoring 15 goals.

City further increased their lead on thirty-two minutes, when Eric Brook made a beautiful centre and Marshall ran through and headed well beyond the reach of Webster. Hardly had the celebrating subsided when City scored again: Billy Felton took a free-kick and, as he lifted the ball in towards the goalmouth, Brook nipped through and finished in wonderful fashion.

City had gained the upper hand and their forwards were, at times, playing some delightful football. In the second half, Swindon were completely besieged, as City added a further six goals. Tommy Tait completed a second-half hat-trick with goals on fifty-one, sixty-two and eighty-nine minutes; Marshall added a further three goals to his personal tally, scoring on fifty-nine, sixty and seventy-one minutes. Morris squeezed a solitary goal in for Swindon on seventy minutes.

As may be imagined, Barber did not have a busy afternoon, but he made one or two good saves, notably from Eddidston in the first half and Morris in the second. Overall, though, it was not a good day for Swindon, but despite being hopelessly out-classed, they never gave up.

Manchester City: Barber, Felton, McCloy, Barrass, Cowan, Heineman, Toseland, Marshall, Tait, Johnson, Brook

Swindon Town: Webster, Penn, Girvan, Low, Humphries, Archer, Denyer, Eddidston, Morris, Roberts, McCartney

Referee: C. Lines (Birmingham)

Season: 1929/30

P	W	D	L	F	A	PTS
42	19	9	14	91	81	47

Division: One
Position: Third
Manager: Peter Hodge
Top Goalscorer: Tommy Tait (31)
Average Attendance: 33,000

Manchester City v. Everton

29 April 1933

FA Cup final
Wembley Stadium, London
Attendance: 92,950

Manchester City 0   Everton 3
                         Stein, Dean, Dunn

When Manchester City and Everton met at Wembley, it was the first time the two clubs had ever met in a FA Cup tie. The fact that two clubs from the north were in the Cup Final was noted by Wembley caterers, who altered their menu to account for the culinary tastes of the supporters of both clubs: they increased their order of pies!

The teams had already met in the League twice during the season, Everton winning 2-1 at Goodison and City winning the return 3-0, so an equal contest was expected.

As is traditional in the build up to major cup finals, City enjoyed some preparation time away from the day-to-day life of Manchester. They spent ten days at Bushey Hall Hotel near Watford, in a team-building exercise aimed at calming everybody's nerves.

City suffered a major blow on the day of the final, losing Fred Tilson, who was still visibly suffering from a mysterious injury to a leg nerve. Bobby Marshall took his place.

Within a matter of seconds, City made their first attack and Everton 'keeper Ted Sagar competently caught a high centre, and this seemed to calm his nerves, as well as those of his fellow players. Len Langford in the City goal was also struggling, but mainly against the strong sunlight, which was shining directly in his face. Every time a high ball came across, he appeared to be blinded by the sun.

There was no score in the game until the fortieth minute, when Everton's Britton forced Langford to look skyward, as he lifted a high ball into the goalmouth. With Dixie Dean in close attendance, Langford missed the ball and it landed at the feet of Jack Stein, who simply tapped it in.

Seven minutes after the interval, Britton sent another high ball into the box and, as Langford tried to catch it, Dean barged into him. The ball came out of the goalkeeper's hands, and both players and the ball ended up in the net – Everton were two-up.

The men from Merseyside scored a third goal, ten minutes from time. Geldard placed a corner kick perfectly for Dunn to head a spectacular goal.

So, it was Dixie Dean who went up to receive the cup from the Duke of York, but Sam Cowan was ever optimistic in defeat and, when he was handed his medal, Cowan replied that he would be back the next year to win the cup.

Manchester City: Langford, Cann, Dale, Busby, Cowan, Bray, Toseland, Marshall, Herd, McMullan, Brook

Everton: Sagar, Cook, Cresswell, Britton, White, Thomson, Geldard, Dunn, Dean, Johnson, Stein

Referee: E. Wood (Sheffield)

Matt Busby signed for City from Denny Hibs and played in 227 games between 1928-1936, scoring 14 goals.

By the time of the 1933 FA Cup final, Matt Busby was established at right-half and reflected on the final in his book, *My Story*, published in 1957:

'The Everton match was lost in the dressing room – of that I am convinced. The Cup Final at Wembley is quite different from any other game of soccer ... because it is at the Empire Stadium that nervous tension reaches its peak. There are ways of combating big match jitters; unfortunately Manchester City employed none of these methods. We turned up at Wembley one hour and three-quarters before kick-off time ... a tactical blunder of the first magnitude. The players took a stroll on to the delightful green turf, surveyed massive terraces...returned to the dressing room and were ready to start the match at 2.15 p.m. With each moment of passing time, the nervous tension increased, and, by the time our captain, Sam Cowan, was summoned to lead us out to meet the Duke of York (later King George VI), we were as unprepared for a game of football as any team could be. City did themselves less than justice on the day. We played badly ... yet how different might the story have been had City not suffered nearly two hours of dressing room agony before it all started. Sam Cowan, as he received his loser's medal from the Duke of York in the Royal Box at Wembley promised, "We'll be back next year Your Highness ... to collect the winning medals."'

Season: 1932/33

P	W	D	L	F	A	PTS
42	16	5	21	68	71	37

Division:	One
Position:	Sixteenth
Manager:	Wilf Wild
Top Goalscorer:	Fred Tilson (23)
Average Attendance:	23,000

S. COWAN.

Left: *Sam Cowan signed for City from Doncaster Rovers and played in 407 games between 1924-1935, scoring 24 goals. Right: A ticket from the Cup Final.*

MANCHESTER CITY V. STOKE CITY

3 March 1934

FA Cup Sixth Round
Maine Road, Manchester
Attendance: 84,569

Manchester City 1   Stoke City 0
Brook

For the first time in the history of Maine Road, the gates had to be closed before the start of a match. A record attendance for any match outside of a Cup Final or international in this country, came to see City battle out a Cup tie against Stoke City.

The Potteries side was not short of support, bringing with them thousands of their own followers. The sheer size of the crowd proved too much for some and, having got in and wandered about looking for somewhere to view the match from, many decided they could not possibly see any of the play and tried to leave the ground. Ambulance men were kept busy and treated some 100 people for injuries and abrasions, caused by the crushing crowd. Three were taken to Manchester Royal Infirmary.

Once the game got under way, City had a difficult start as Stoke kept them under pressure. In the first minute of the match, Stoke had a double-barrelled chance to strike what might have been a decisive blow. Johnson put a ball across, and all that was required was a simple tap into the net, but first Sale, and then a seventeen-year-old Stanley Matthews, contrived to miss it.

The only goal of the game came after fifteen minutes. Eric Brook received the ball out on the touchline, in what appeared to be a harmless position. He swung over a high ball, clearly intended for one of City's forwards. The ball appeared to be going out of play and 'keeper Roy John, under pressure from Fred Tilson, was in position to catch it. However, as the ball came down, it swerved, apparently caught by the wind, and it passed through his hands and into the top corner of the net.

With the sun and wind at their backs in the second half, City were a different team, and, although Stoke made a gallant fight of it, they had to rely on John to keep the margin down. Stoke launched one last flurry and, in the final minute of the game, were awarded a corner. Everybody bar the Stoke 'keeper was in the box; fortunately for City, Stokes centre half Arthur Turner headed the ball a fraction over the bar.

A few seconds later, the whistle went, and City were through to the semi-final of the FA Cup for the third consecutive season. A record crowd had witnessed Brook score the only goal of the game, and people talked for weeks as to whether or not he meant it.

Manchester City: Swift, Barnett, Dale, Busby, Cowan, Bray, Toseland, Marshall, Tilson, Herd, Brook

Stoke City: John, McGrory, Spencer, Tutin, Turner, Sellars, Matthews, Lidde, Sale, Davies, Johnson

Against Stoke, Frank Swift, who had been on trial from Fleetwood weeks earlier, was playing his sixteenth game for the club, after stepping up from the third team, with regular 'keepers Len Langford and Louis Barber out injured. This 1-0 triumph put City in the semi-finals, a match in which Matt Busby recalled, 'Swift was still a very raw boy as he took the field against Aston Villa, our last opponents before Wembley. That day against Villa, in the early minutes of the game, Frank Swift really looked a goalkeeper … City won 6-1 and Swifty earned himself a Cup Final job.'

Season: 1933/34

P	W	D	L	F	A	PTS
42	17	11	14	65	72	45

Division: One
Position: Fifth
Manager: Wilf Wild
Top Goalscorer: Alex Herd (21)
Average Attendance: 28,000

Cartoon taken from The Athletic News.

MANCHESTER CITY V. PORTSMOUTH

28 April 1934

FA Cup Final
Wembley Stadium, London
Attendance: 93,258

Manchester City 2   Portsmouth 1
Tilson (2)   *Rutherford*

After the disappointment of losing the 1933 FA Cup final to Everton, and to try and change their Cup luck, the Blues spent a week at The Palace Hotel, Birkdale, Southport, prior to travelling down to Wembley.

Blues captain Sam Cowan made a vow that City would return to Wembley and, sure enough, they did. Having already suffered the bitter taste of a Cup Final defeat, the Blues were reluctant to fritter away another chance.

Two of City's most influential players almost missed the final, but for contrasting reasons. Cowan was suffering with a septic toe, which he was fearful of telling any City officials about, in case he missed the final, and Alex Herd was allegedly so enthralled by an Edgar Wallace thriller that he was left behind in the dressing room just before the game was due to begin.

The game itself was an action-packed affair from the start. Eric Brook missed a glorious opportunity to give City the lead, shooting wide from a free kick. A young and nervous Frank Swift, in goals for City had to be alert at all times especially when Smith and Rutherford had chances to open the scoring.

Portsmouth scored first, just before the half-hour mark. Accepting a pass from Weddle,

City players relax at the Palace Hotel before the 1934 Cup Final.

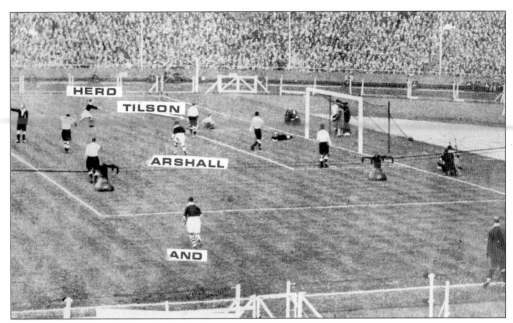

Tilson strikes on of his brace.

Rutherford struck a long low shot that eluded Swift, the City 'keeper only getting his finger tips to it.

The score remained 1-0 at half time, with Swift blaming himself for the goal. Rutherford then missed a chance to put the game beyond City, and when Alex Herd hit a post for City, it seemed their luck was not to be.

Then, on seventy-five minutes, City fought their way back into the game. From a corner, Sam Cowan collided with Portsmouth's Jimmy Allen. The clash was so serious that Allen had to leave the field of play for treatment, and City took advantage of this. Fred Tilson received the ball from Brook and went on a meandering run down the left wing, finally screwed a left shot past the advancing Gilfillan into the Portsmouth goal.

As the tension rose in the final minutes, Brook made another telling pass, which Tilson accepted, and he decisively swept the ball into the net. City had the lead for the first time.

The dying seconds seemed to last an eternity, but sheer graft and determination helped City through to the final whistle. As it blew, an amusing incident happened: Swift turned to collect his cap and gloves and promptly fainted. The victory was all too much for him.

Sam Cowan collected the cup from King George V, the first time they had won it in thirty years, and the streets of Manchester were thronged with people the following day as they welcomed their heroes home.

Manchester City: Swift, Barnett, Dale, Busby, Cowan, Bray, Toseland, Marshall, Tilson, Herd, Brook

Portsmouth: Gilfillan, Mackie, W Smith, Nichol, Allen, Thackeray, Worrall, J Smith, Weddle, Easson, Rutherford

Referee: S.F. Rous (Herts)

Matt Busby recalled in *My Story* that City's preparations and relaxed manner for the 1934 Final could not have been different from the previous season:

'The team arrived barely an hour before kick-off and had a happy-go-lucky approach to the game. There were no nerves, there was no bickering or snapping at colleagues; just complete harmony and eagerness to get on with the job on hand. As the City and Portsmouth players were being introduced to King George V before the Cup Final, the King noticed that our centre forward, Fred Tilson, was wearing a knee bandage. "What is wrong with your knee?" he asked. "Your Majesty," interrupted Sam Cowan, "apart from a broken knee, a bad back, and a touch of pneumonia, Fred's in perfect health."'

As for the match, Busby recalled, 'It was a testing time for the boy Swift ... Frank should have saved an early shot from Pompey left-winger Rutherford, which gave our opponents the lead. For the rest of the match, we were the better side, but not until about twenty minutes from full time did things turn in our favour. Fred Tilson equalized from the edge of the penalty area and, a few moments later, scored the winning goal from almost the same spot.

'While all this was happening, Frank Swift was virtually a spectator but, after Tilson's second goal, there was a brief Pompey revival. Jack Smith went through our defence, and, as Swifty came out, hit a magnificent shot with "goal" written all over it. Frank made a save I shall always remember, and a few minutes later, the Cup was in the keeping of Manchester City.'

Manchester City proudly display the FA Cup in 1934. From left to right, back row (directors): R. Smith, W. Shaw, H. Wood, Dr J. Holmes. Third row: W. Wild (secretary-manager), A. Alexander (director), M. Busby, F. Swift, L. Barnett, J. Bray, A. Bell (trainer). Second row: F. Tilson, W. Dale, S. Cowan (captain), A. Hughes (chairman), R. Marshall, A. Herd, J. McLuckie. Front row (on ground): E. Toseland, E. Brook.

Programme for the 1934 Cup Final.

Manchester City v. Sheffield Wednesday

24 April 1937

Football League First Division
Maine Road, Manchester
Attendance: 55,000

Manchester City 4	Sheffield Wednesday 1
Brook (2)	*Rimmer*
Tilson, Doherty	

The season that ended with the greatest prize in English football could not have started in a less convincing way. Just days before Christmas, City were languishing near the bottom of the table, and had all ready suffered at the hands of Sheffield Wednesday, losing 1-5, with Peter Doherty scoring City's only goal.

Four months on, and Sheffield Wednesday visited Maine Road for the penultimate game of the season. The Blues needed two points from their last two games to clinch the title, and Wednesday had to win to have any chance of survival in the top division.

City went into this game unbeaten in 20 successive league games. They were determined to win the Championship for the first time in front of their home supporters, and, not surprisingly, they were the hot favourites.

The Blues' start to the game was a little tentative early on, but their nerves settled in the nineteenth minute. John Percival passed to Doherty, who in turn found Eric Brook, who lashed in an unstoppable shot from a difficult angle, to give City the lead.

They then continued to set about Wednesday, and five minutes later Fred Tilson doubled the lead after being put through by Doherty. Then, on thirty-one minutes, came a goal from Doherty that literally brought the house down, and the game was all but over.

A towering clearance from Frank Swift led to Doherty gaining possession in the centre of the

Manchester City FC, 1936/37.

field. A brisk interchange of passes with Tilson carved open the Wednesday defence. The Sheffield defenders were helpless to intercept, and Doherty applied the final touch, as the ball finally came to rest in the corner of the net.

That was Doherty's twenty-ninth goal of the season, and one of the finest Maine Road had ever seen. It was a superb goal, which was the product of splendid team work.

The crowd rose to their feet to give the team a standing ovation, as they left the field of play at the half-time interval.

Wednesday pulled a consolation goal back through Rimmer in the second half, but a last-minute goal from Brook, his second of the game, meant that the Championship had been won, putting the crowd in just the right mood for the celebrations that were about to begin. The final whistle went: City had done it, and a joyous pitch invasion began. Manchester City were Champions for the first time in their history.

In all that was going on, nobody spared a thought for Sheffield Wednesday, who had just been relegated.

Manchester City: Swift, Clarke, Barkas, Percival, Marshall, Bray, Toseland, Herd, Tilson, Doherty, Brook

Sheffield Wednesday: Smith, Ashley, Catlin, Grosvenor, Hanford, Burrows, Luke, Robinson, Dewar, Drury, Rimmer

Referee: R.W. Blake (Middlesbrough)

Peter Doherty recalled this triumph in an interview in 1968, 'City were a top-class side in the thirties, but despite the title win, City were not a great club. They lacked foresight, and it possibly proved their undoing for the many lean years which were to follow. We had a side to be proud of though. There were potential scorers in the attack all the time – men like Brook, Herd and Tilson. Even I was collecting around the 30-goal mark in those seasons. Tilson wasn't a great player, but he had a terrific lot of craft, and was very brainy, and this compensated for the lack of other qualities. Brook had two great feet and Herd was the type of player who could whip them home from 30 to 40 yards – it never seemed too difficult for him. The spirit of our Championship side was marvellous. That team played some marvellous football, with an ability in the side of getting goals from any source.'

Season: 1936/37

P	W	D	L	F	A	PTS
42	22	13	7	107	61	57

Division: One
Position: First
Manager: Wilf Wild
Top Goalscorer: Peter Doherty (32)
Average Attendance: 34,000

TRANMERE ROVERS V. MANCHESTER CITY

26 & 27 December 1938

Football League Second Division
Prenton Park, Tranmere
Attendance 14,006

Tranmere Rovers 3	Manchester City 9
Docking (2)	*Milsom (4)*
Travis	*Toseland (2), Doherty (2)*
	Herd

Football League Division Two
Maine Road, Manchester
Attendance: 43,994

Manchester City 5	Tranmere Rovers 2
Milsom (3)	*Docking (pen), Miller (pen)*
Doherty, Pritchard	

A poor start to the season saw some City supporters attack the direction of the club, sending letters to the 'Blind Asylum', c/o Maine Road. An upturn in fortunes saw City climb the table, but never really challenge for promotion. This particular season saw two remarkable games played over the Christmas period when Jackie Milsom, signed from Bolton Wanderers in February 1938, scored seven times in two days, in the thrashings handed out to Tranmere Rovers.

The first game at Birkenhead was marred after twenty-two minutes by a serious injury to Wassall, Tranmere's right-back, who, in a collision with Les McDowall, received a double compound fracture to the right leg. The incident was so severe that it caused a number of men and women to faint. At this point in the match, the scores were level. Docking's goal for Tranmere on eleven minutes was cancelled out by Jack Milsom's goal after fifteen minutes. It was not surprising, on the heavy ground, that City had matters more or less their own way and, before the half-time interval, they had scored an additional two goals, Alec Herd (thirty-two minutes) and Ernie Toseland (thirty-five minutes).

More goals followed shortly after the commencement of the second half, Peter Doherty got the Blues' fifth on fifty-two minutes, and the sixth arrived moments later from Milsom. It was Tranmere's turn to score then, with Docking's second goal of the game. At this point, City also had the misfortune of losing a player, Eric Brook having to leave the field with a pulled thigh muscle. Further goals followed through Milsom (sixty-seven), Doherty (eighty), Toseland (eighty-five), Milsom (eighty-seven) and, finally, a consolation goal from Travis in the final minute.

Jack Milsom signed for City from Bolton Wanderers and played in 36 games between 1938-1940 scoring 24 goals.

By scoring five goals in the return match at Maine Road, City brought their tally against Tranmere in the two holiday matches to 14 goals against 5. City were aggressive from the start and Milsom scored twice before half time. Docking pulled one back for the Rovers from the penalty spot and, although City had numerous chances afterwards, they wasted many more, and further goals from Jack Pritchard, Milsom and Doherty did not represent their true superiority. Miller scored for Tranmere from another penalty kick.

The season ended with City in fifth position and, considering their start, this was a respectable position. With their total of 96 League goals, they had scored more than any other club during the season.

Game 1

Tranmere Rovers: Curnow, Wassall, Owen, Davies, Anderson, Day, Dellow, Miller, Travis, Docking, Roy

Manchester City: Swift, Sproston, Westwood, Percival, Cardwell, McDowall, Toseland, Herd, Milsom, Doherty, Pritchard

Game 2

Manchester City: Swift, Sproston, Westwood, Percival, Cardwell, McDowall, Toseland, Herd, Milsom, Doherty, Pritchard

Programme for 1938 Manchester City v. Tranmere Rovers.

Tranmere Rovers: Curnow, Anderson, Jones, Davies, Walkden, Day, Dellow, Miller, Travis, Docking, Roy

Season: 1938/39

P	W	D	L	F	A	PTS
42	21	7	14	96	72	49

Division:	Two
Position:	Fifth
Manager:	Wilf Wild
Top Goalscorer:	Alex Herd (22)
Average Attendance:	29,000

MANCHESTER CITY V. WEST HAM UNITED

24 May 1947

Football League Second Division
Maine Road, Manchester
Attendance: 31,980

Manchester City 2   West Ham United 0
McDowall, Smith

In their quest for the Second Division Championship, it was essential that City beat West Ham United at Maine Road. Victory would virtually assure them of the Championship.

For the first few minutes, West Ham gave the City defence some trouble. The Hammers were playing an open game on a pitch that was not easy to play on, dry and bumpy with a cross-wind making ball control difficult. City, however, countered in style. Walker was penalized for handling six yards outside the penalty area, but the free-kick came to nothing. Neither side found it easy to control the ball, due to the condition of the pitch and, in the next City attack, Andy Black picked up a centre from Maurice Dunkley and sent the ball wide.

The City defence were left in a tangle, after a smart interchange of passes between Woodgate and Parsons saw Woodgate strike the side netting with his shot. After twenty-one minutes, City made their first serious attack. Alec Herd, Black and Dunkley shared a move down the centre, and when Black was on the point of shooting, he was brought down in the penalty area. Centre half Les McDowall took the penalty kick, and was a surprised man when the ball found the net. Placing his shot to Ernie Gregory's right, he saw the ball strike the foot of the post and rebound into the net.

It was not until the second half that City's attack came into its own, and George Smith settled the game for City with fifteen minutes left. Smith collected a long pass from Black; he dribbled the ball into the penalty area and hit a terrific shot past Gregory.

Although the football never reached great heights, City dominated the game with a workman-like performance and deserved the vital points. However, City then lost their next two matches at Sheffield Wednesday (0-1) and West Bromwich Albion (1-3). The season actually ended on 14 June 1947, and the final match was a strange one for a couple of reasons. George Smith scored all five goals against Newport to finish top scorer for the season, and equalled Tommy Johnson's record of most goals in a single match, and Roy Clarke made his debut for City. Clarke was in the middle of achieving the unusual feat of playing consecutive games in three different divisions. His previous game had been for Cardiff City in the Third Division (South) and his next match was in the First Division.

The Blues won the Second Division title for the fifth time with 62 points, four more than second-placed Burnley. City were back in the First Division.

Official programme for theManchester City v. West Ham match.

Manchester City: Thurlow, Sproston, Barkas, Fagan, McDowall, Emptage, Dunkley, Herd, Black, Smith, Westwood

West Ham United: Gregory, Corbett, Devlin, Cater, Walker, Small, Woodgate, Parsons, Travis, Wood, Bainbridge

Referee: G.S. Blackhall (Wednesbury)

New signing, at the time, Roy Clarke recalled, 'I signed for City the day before their penultimate game of the season at home to West Ham, as the Second Division title beckoned in May 1947. I was invited to their team meeting and sat in the corner; there were stars everywhere including the great Frank Swift. I thought I'd hear amazing words of wisdom. The manager, Sam Cowan, walked in and picked up the ball. "Hello lads," he bounced the ball on the floor, "okay, we're playing West Ham today … get stuck in!"… then walked out. That was it; I couldn't believe it!'

Season: 1946/47

P	W	D	L	F	A	PTS
42	26	10	6	78	35	62

Division:	Two
Position:	First
Manager:	Wilf Wild/Sam Cowan
Top Goalscorer:	George Smith (23)
Average Attendance:	37,695

Team picture, 1946/47. From left to right, back row: Stroston, Smith, Walsh, Black, Cardwell. Front row: Dunkerley, McDowall, Swift, Jackson, Rudd, Barkas.

PRESTON NORTH END V. MANCHESTER CITY

21 August 1954

Football League First Division
Deepdale, Preston
Attendance: 35,000

Preston North End 5   Manchester City 0
Wayman (3)
Baxter, Foster

For several seasons, City had struggled in the League, but manager Les McDowall had different ideas for the season ahead. He introduced a new tactical ploy which had been tried out by the reserves. It had also been used successfully by the Hungarians in defeating England in the fifties, and had proved totally confusing to the opposition. City introduced 'The Revie Plan,' which came into force at Preston.

Manchester City supporters rallied together in their thousands for the club's opening game at Deepdale, and they awaited with interest, the continuation of the plan. It was to be a hard task, as City had been beaten soundly on their two previous visits: 2-6 in the 1952/53 season and 0-4 the following season.

The opening minutes of the game were played at top speed, and North End were quickly on the attack. In the ninth minute, they took the lead, Foster drew the City defence and his pass found Baxter in such a good position, that he only had to take a couple of strides forward, before slamming the ball past a helpless Bert Trautmann. The ever-struggling City defence gradually wilted under the pressure, but, such was the performance of City's German 'keeper that it was not until eighteen minutes before the end of the game that Foster added the second goal to make the score 2-0 in Preston's favour.

Then Wayman, who had been limping for some time, enhanced his reputation as an opportunist by scoring three goals in ten minutes. Two of those came when Bill Leivers was receiving attention on the touchline. The City defence were too occupied coping with the nimble forwards of North End to produce any opportunities for City's attacking play, and any threats they made were isolated. Preston were in irresistible mood, so any harsh criticism City received after the match could not be really justified. City eventually finished the season in seventh place and the 'Revie plan' ended up taking them to Wembley.

Roy Little recalled: 'This match was the start of my career at City, and the era in which we played to the 'Revie plan'. Don had been bought as a wing-half, but wasn't the best defensive tackler. However he was a great passer of the ball, so he played as the link-man, and it worked brilliantly. I didn't play against Preston, but I came into the side with Ken Barnes, because Bill Leivers and Ken McTavish got injured. The system began to

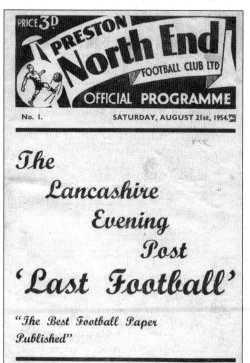

Preston North End v. Man. City programme.

work, and we went on a great run that season. We had the right players for the system and we just gelled.'

Preston North End:
Thompson, Cunningham, Walton, Docherty, Marston, Forbes, Finney, Foster, Wayman, Baxter, Morrison

Manchester City:
Trautmann, Leivers, Meadows, McTavish, Ewing, Paul, Spurdle, McAdams, Revie, Hart, Clarke

Referee: J.H. Clough (Bolton)

In 1954/55, the first team employed a new tactic: the 'Revie plan', in which Ken Barnes played a key role. 'Les McDowell experimented with different formations, but this was the most famous one. Originally, I played this system in the reserves with Johnny Williamson; and we didn't lose for 30-odd games. The first team tried it at the start of 1954/55 at Preston; and we lost 0-5! However, we persevered, and it brought a lot of success. Defences were used to a big centre forward like Nat Lofthouse or Trevor Ford staying up, it was a real battle. Against us, our centre forward, Don Revie, would play deeper and come at them; not be with them all the time, so the centre halves had nobody to mark. We played the ball in the middle of the park and started linking up: Don, me at wing half, our inside forwards and our wingers would alternate, and it caused problems. When I was running towards our box and saw the ball coming over, I knew Bert would gather it, so I'd turn the other way to attack. Bert would come out, saying "here have it", and I'd be on my way linking up. Going forward with the attack was a piece of cake as far as I was concerned. I loved the system.'

Don Revie signed for City from Hull City and played in 178 games between 1951-1956, scoring 41 goals.

63

Manchester United v. Manchester City

12 February 1955

Football League First Division
Old Trafford, Manchester
Attendance: 47,914

Manchester United 0   Manchester City 5
                        Fagan (2), Hayes (2)
                        Hart

One of the greatest delights of watching football is derby days and in this season the blue half of Manchester had the superior hand with three games, three victories.

The first came in a 3-2 league victory at Maine Road, when goals from Billy McAdams, Paddy Fagan and Johnny Hart secured victory in an outstanding game. City had relied on secure, well-organised teamwork and a patient build-up to acquire their goals.

The two teams also met in the FA Cup at Maine Road, and goals from Joe Hayes and Don Revie ensured victory in a splendid Cup tie that would be remembered for years to come by all who were fortunate enough to be present.

Two weeks later, the teams were meeting in a return League game at Old Trafford. United were the talk of football, and the public flocked to Old Trafford, thrilled by the skills and attacking nature of the 'Busby Babes.'

On a cold winter's day with the pitch frozen down one side, United opted to play an all-out attacking plan and apply pressure to try and offset the famous 'Revie plan', but to little effect. City scored their first goal of the game on fifteen minutes, when Johnny Hart latched on to a Don Revie ball into the box and fired past Ray Wood.

The United plan nearly succeeded in the last twenty minutes of the first half. They had City defending desperately and, with a bit of luck, could have scored three goals. It was not to be their day however, and, on fifty-eight minutes, City scored a second when, after an interchange of passes,

Manchester City FC, c.1955.

Paddy Fagan found himself in the clear. From that point on, City played United out of the game. The Blues poured forward, and Joe Hayes struck home a third goal. A fourth was soon to arrive, again as a result of the 'Revie plan'. Hayes reached a Roy Clarke pass, and swept the ball past Wood, for his second of the game.

Allenby Chilton tried valiantly to rouse his fading players but, with the defence fading into complete disorder, Fagan completed the rout by scoring a fifth and final goal.

Both teams deserved the highest praise for a thriller on a pitch that did not really invite entertaining football. The 'Revie Plan' had completely bamboozled United for a third time.

City were clearly the Champions of Manchester, there was no doubting their supremacy.

Manchester United: Wood, Foulkes, Byrne, Gibson, Chilton, Whitefoot, Berry, Blanchflower, Webster, Edwards, Pegg

Manchester City: Trautmann, Meadows, Little, Barnes, Ewing, Paul, Fagan, Hayes, Revie, Hart, Clarke

Referee: G. Black (Kendal)

Roy Little recalled, 'This was the third time we had played them that season, because we beat them in the cup 2-0 a couple of weeks earlier, and we were playing some tremendous stuff. Also, this was the era of the "Busby Babes", so it was a terrific performance. It was certainly the best away result of my career! Because of the Cup defeat, Matt Busby changed his formation. Matt thought we were weaker in midfield, only having two players there, and moved Duncan Edwards to inside forward, which was a mistake. Duncan was a powerhouse of a player, and was awesome going forward, but at inside forward he was receiving the ball rather than distributing it. Though undoubtedly a great player, his one weak point was turning sharply, and that day he definitely played out of position, which helped us.'

Season: 1954/55

P	W	D	L	F	A	PTS
42	18	10	14	76	69	46

Division:	One
Position:	Seventh
Manager:	Les McDowall
Top Goalscorer:	Johnny Hart/Joe Hayes (15)
Average Attendance:	35,165

Manchester City v. Sunderland

26 March 1955

FA Cup semi-final
Villa Park, Birmingham
Attendance: 58,498

Manchester City 1   Sunderland 0
Clarke

Torrential rain, over a period of twenty-four hours, almost forced the postponement of this FA Cup semi-final clash with Sunderland. Such was the severity of the rain at Villa Park, that the match was in doubt just thirty minutes before the kick-off. Large pools of water were dotted liberally all over the playing surface, especially down the middle of the pitch, from goalmouth to goalmouth. The final go-ahead for the game was given by the senior linesman, as the referee was delayed by huge traffic jams, as were many supporters, whose travel plans had been thrown into disarray as they trekked miles through the rain to get to the game.

    City were the first team out on to the pitch, and emerged to a great burst of cheering from some 25,000 wet and bedraggled City supporters. The team were sporting their new all-blue kit, purchased for them by a local businessman.

    Minutes into the game, conditions were so appalling that it was virtually impossible to pass the ball along the ground. The state of the ground placed more emphasis on the physical attributes of the players, rather than their skills. City opened brightly, and a corner for the Blues in the opening minutes set the whole place alight with excitement, although the set piece came to nothing.

    Sunderland eventually set their sights on goal, with a combined attack from Bingham and Fleming, but their efforts were ruled offside. The non-stop action continued, and City mounted two further glorious attacks on the Sunderland goal. Paddy Fagan mesmerised the defence with an excellent dribble in tight space, which Fraser was very fortunate to turn away at the second attempt. The second attack saw Roy Clarke send in an angled drive from 15 yards, which Fraser pulled down, almost on the line.

    Both teams continued to produce first-class entertainment and plenty of good football, in spite of the really atrocious ground and weather conditions. On fifty-six minutes, the game produced its one and only goal. A free-kick, taken out on the right, sailed over the head of Bobby Johnstone, Roy Clarke dived forwards and headed towards the left of 'keeper Willie Fraser. The ball hit the net, but it seemed to take a few seconds for anyone in the crowd to realize what had happened.

    City were back at Wembley, and all twenty-two players deserved the highest commendation for their grit under difficult conditions.

Semi-final programme.

Manchester City: Trautmann, Meadows, Little, Barnes, Ewing, Paul, Fagan, Hayes, Revie, Johnstone, Clarke

Sunderland: Fraser, Hedley, McDonald, Anderson, Daniel, Aitken, Bingham, Fleming, Purdon, Shackleton, Elliott

Referee: F.B. Coultas (Hull)

Roy Little recalled, 'Mud, mud, glorious mud! Sunderland had good ball players in Len Shackleton and Billy Bingham. When we arrived, we went to the dressing room and, at about 2.15 p.m., the referee came in. He told us he would have to inspect the pitch because of torrential rain, and said it was a probability that the game would be called off. The pitch was a bog; he was out there about fifteen minutes. He came back to the dressing rooms and told us the game was on. We couldn't believe it … it wasn't playable. Apparently, because it had been raining so hard, they allowed the fans in to get out of the rain, so they couldn't really call it off, it was Hobson's choice. As it happens, the conditions suited us better. One player Roy Paul hated playing against was Len Shackleton, who was a real ball player, and the conditions ruined his game that day.'

The semi-final would bring both elation and heartbreak for Roy Clarke. Elation because his goal sent the team to Wembley, but also heartbreak because an injury would cost him his place in the final itself. Here, Wally Barnes and John McTavish help Roy from the field after he sustained his injury.

Manchester City v. Newcastle United

7 May 1955

FA Cup final
Wembley Stadium
Attendance: 100,000

Manchester City 1	Newcastle United 3
Johnstone	*Milburn, Mitchell, Hannah*

It was the first time in over twenty years that City had reached the final of the FA Cup. In reaching the final, they had beaten a number of leading teams, including their local rivals, Manchester United, at Old Trafford.

For this particular final, the Blues were making a little bit of history. The team included the first German to play in a Wembley cup final (Bert Trautmann) and the first Channel Islander (Billy Spurdle). City were also the first finalists to wear track suits when they stepped out in front of a capacity crowd at Wembley. There was also the small matter of who would be fit to play. The squad was already missing Roy Clarke and Johnny Hart, and there was a doubt over Trautmann's fitness. Other talking points included an argument over poor seat allocations to club officials, and whether or not City would implement the 'Revie Plan.'

When the game started, Newcastle galloped towards the City goal. Jackie Milburn forced a corner off Dave Ewing and, from the corner kick, White placed the ball perfectly for Milburn, who was running into the box. He headed in powerfully, the ball going into the net off the underside of the bar. Incredibly, City were a goal down after forty-five seconds. Worse was to follow for City in the nineteenth minute, when Jimmy Meadows badly damaged his right knee in turning to tackle Newcastle's winger, Bobby Mitchell. Such was the damage to his knee ligaments, that he never played football again. The injury meant that the Blues faced playing the remaining seventy-odd minutes with ten men. They rallied, and before half time had their best period of the game, which resulted in Bobby Johnstone scoring with a wonderful header from a Joe Hayes cross, and City went in at the interval on level terms.

The second forty-five-minute spell brought two further goals for Newcastle. Eight minutes into the half, Mitchell gave Newcastle the lead, scoring with a shot that beat Trautmann at the near post. In the fifty-ninth minute, another Mitchell shot was parried by Trautmann, and George Hannah, who later went on to make 131 League and Cup appearances for City, followed up to make it three.

City could find no way back, so the first Cup Final to be shown on television involving City saw a third FA Cup victory for Newcastle in a five-year period.

Manchester City: Trautmann, Meadows, Little, Barnes, Ewing, Paul, Spurdle, Hayes, Revie, Johnstone, Fagan

Newcastle United: Simpson, Cowell, Batty, Scoular, Stokoe, Casey, White, Milburn, Keeble, Hannah, Mitchell

Referee: R.J. Leafe (Nottingham)

Ken Barnes recalled, 'Of course we were disappointed. Jackie Milburn headed their first; Roy Paul was marking him and couldn't believe it because Milburn had never headed a goal like that in his life. We equalized, but after Jimmy Meadows got injured, that was it really, they came more into the game and it became very difficult for us.'

Bobby Johnstone signed for City from Hibernian and played in 139 games between 1955-1959, scoring 51 goals.

Manchester City v. Birmingham City

5 May 1956

FA Cup Final
Wembley Stadium, London
Attendance: 100,000

Manchester City 3	Birmingham City 1
Hayes	*Kinsey*
Dyson	
Johnstone	

Club captain Roy Paul vowed that he would lead his team back to Wembley after the disappointment of suffering defeat against Newcastle United the previous season. This time, his team was going to win the cup.

City had travelled down the week prior to the game, and spent ten days on the south coast at Eastbourne. The late withdrawal of Billy Spurdle meant Don Revie was in the team, and Wembley spectators would, yet again, get the chance to see the much-criticized 'Revie Plan,' a tactic whereby the centre forward lies deep to feed the forwards. There was also no place for Johnny Hart, who must have felt he was the unluckiest person in the world, especially after he had missed the previous year's Cup Final with a broken leg.

City made a dream start to the game. Three minutes in, City, in what at the time was an unfamiliar maroon-and-white striped kit, were a goal up. Revie swept the ball out to Roy Clarke on the left wing, who then found Revie again with a pass which he flicked through his legs towards Joe Hayes, and he scored with a left shot into the corner of the net. Twelve minutes later, Birmingham were level, Noel Kinsey's shot going in via a post. The scoreline remained the same until half time.

In the second half, City played so well that they could have had four or five goals, but settled for second-half strikes from Jack Dyson and Bobby Johnstone within the space of three minutes. From a throw-in, there was some neat inter-passing involving three players, Johnstone, Ken Barnes and Revie, which gave Dyson a clear run on goal to score. Johnstone then put the game beyond doubt; and, incident-ally, his goal put him in the record books as the first person to score in successive FA Cup finals.

Then an incident occurred which would be remembered for all time. With seventeen minutes of the game left, Bert Trautmann thwarted a Birmingham attack, and in doing

Bert Trautmann is helped from the field clearly in pain.

Roy Paul delivers his promise…

so, his bravery at diving at the feet of Peter Murphy led to the diagnosis of a broken neck in tests carried out days after the final. At the time, the severity of the injury was not known so, after lengthy treatment, Bert courageously continued the game, although he was in obvious pain. He even went onto collect his Cup Winners' medal and then joined his colleagues for a celebration banquet at the Café Royal, London. However, his injury meant that he was then unable to play for seven months.

So, against all the odds and blighted by injury, City battled to a magnificent victory. Winning the FA Cup has to be every club's major aim, and this game can be considered the game of a lifetime. The story of the battle is part of soccer history and City fans will remember it for a very long time.

Manchester City: Trautmann, Leivers, Little, Barnes, Ewing, Paul, Johnstone, Hayes, Revie, Dyson, Clarke

Birmingham City: Merrick, Hall, Green, Newman, Smith, Boyd, Astall, Kinsey, Brown, Murphy, Govan

Referee: A. Bond (London)

Roy Little recalled, 'As a player, you get used to a set pre-match build up, but for a Cup Final, it's really different. The build-up is fantastic and local expectations are huge. Standing in the tunnel before the match is really nerve-racking, although the noise isn't too bad, but, as you walk into the stadium, the feeling as the noise hits you, is awesome, it's impossible to describe fully. It's just incredible. At Wembley, everything is vast, it's away from you. Having been there the year before, we knew the format of the day, and it did help. The biggest problem is the timetable because it gives the players very little time to warm up, what with meeting Royalty and so on. As for the match, we played well and should have won more comfortably. Birmingham tried to alter their formation to compete against Don Revie, but failed. Don dominated the game that day, and was deservedly man of the match, he had so much room and space it was unbelievable. As for Bert's injury, it was right in front of me and it was an accident. Murphy couldn't be blamed, he just caught him with his knee as he went for the ball. At the time, we obviously had no idea it was as serious as it was, but he still made important saves afterwards. It was an incredible performance by him when you think about it.

Although we won quite comfortably, having lost at the end of the match the previous year, the main feeling was one of relief in many ways, but we did deserve the win. Naturally the celebrations were better in '56! I remember the previous year, the train stopped at Wilmslow; in '56 we stopped at Piccadilly, and it took longer to get from Piccadilly station to the Town Hall than from Wilmslow the previous year. Wonderful memories.'

Roy Clarke recalled, 'During the team talk, Les McDowell reminded us not to "carry the ball too much", because the pitch could sap your energy, he emphasized, "tire the ball out ... not yourselves". Then it was time to go. When we left the dressing room, I knew we'd go back as winners. Waiting in the tunnel was the worst part; I was petrified. As usual, I was behind Roy and he was really fired up, I can still see him shaking his fist to encourage us, I think it unnerved the Birmingham players!

The noise was incredible as we walked out. The nerves completely went when the match started. Even though you knew you were playing at Wembley, you had to concentrate as if it were just another match. Normally, being on the wing you'd cop the lot, whether it was from

fans, the manager, trainer, reserves. However, at Wembley you can only hear shouting, not who they're shouting for, so I just told myself they were shouting for me and took it as encouragement.

Joe's goal was a shining example of the 'Revie Plan.' Bert moved the ball to Don via Bill Leivers and Ken Barnes. Don then played it 40 yards to me, shouting 'hang on', because he wanted the return. Their full-back was coming over and I thought 'come on, Don ...'. He went past me, and I played the ball just inside a diagonal to him. He ran over it, flicked it between his legs to Joe Hayes, who knocked it in the far corner ... so simple, yet brilliant. In the second half, we got on top and should have scored a few more. We were knocking the ball about and they tired; experience told in the end.'

City legend Frank Swift commented in his newspaper column, 'The boil that kept Bill Spurdle out of the Cup Final turned out to be a blessing in disguise for Manchester City. It allowed manager Les McDowell to field both

Winning at Wembley – such a wonderful spectacle.

Programme for the final.

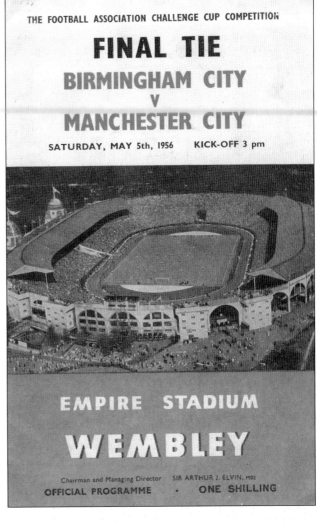

THE FOOTBALL ASSOCIATION CHALLENGE CUP COMPETITION

FINAL TIE

BIRMINGHAM CITY
v
MANCHESTER CITY

SATURDAY, MAY 5th, 1956   KICK-OFF 3 pm

EMPIRE STADIUM

WEMBLEY

Chairman and Managing Director   SIR ARTHUR J. ELVIN, MBE
OFFICIAL PROGRAMME   ·   ONE SHILLING

Bobby Johnstone and Don Revie in his Wembley attack – and these were the two who, more than any others, upset the form book that had made Birmingham the hottest favourites in years... It was obvious from the start, that the team with the jitters was Birmingham. Even so, they had plenty of time to settle, before Manchester turned on the heat that made the second half a one-horse race and a football exhibition. Well done, Manchester. You are worthy Cup-holders!'

Harry Ditton wrote, 'Long after the glory of the pageantry, which makes Wembley such a wonderful spectacle, has been forgotten, they will recall the 1956 Cup Final. It was the sort of game that will live – and deserve to live – in the memory for months, possibly years to come. This was a titanic struggle, which had almost everything – high drama, tension that at times was almost electrical, an abundance of brilliant footcraft, and four goals. Manchester City were not only thoroughly worthy winners, but they maintained the great Wembley tradition of a side never losing the second time when they have appeared there in successive seasons.'

Season: 1955/56

P	W	D	L	F	A	PTS
42	18	10	14	82	69	46

Division: One
Position: Fourth
Manager: Les McDowall
Top Goalscorer: Joe Hayes (27)
Average Attendance: 32,110

73

Manchester City v. Newcastle United

9 January 1957

FA Cup Third Round Replay
Maine Road, Manchester
Attendance: 46,988

Manchester City 4	Newcastle United 5
Johnstone (2)	*White (2)*
Fagan	*Casey (pen)*
Stokoe (og)	*Tait, Curry*

The FA Cup brought together Newcastle United, arguably one of the most successful teams of the 1950s, and City, the current holders of the trophy. Both teams had already played in a thrilling 1-1 draw at Newcastle, so, what promised to be the game of the year, turned out to be one of the most dramatic Cup games in the history of the competition, when it went to extra time.

The opening minutes were to set a precedent for the game. A flying header from Paddy Fagan went narrowly over, but with a bit more luck, it might have gone in. Newcastle replied sharply and Curry sent a shot over the bar.

City's emphasis was on attack. It was a policy that paid off, and Newcastle were a goal down on six minutes. An own goal by Bob Stokoe had started the scoring. Two further goals quickly

Left: Manchester City v. Newcastle United match programme. Right: Roy Little. He joined City from Greenwich Victoria in August 1949. Cool under pressure and with good distribution skills, he was an important member of the City side that reached successive Cup Finals. Roy played 187 times at full-back for City, scoring just twice.

74

followed, Bobby Johnstone headed home a Roy Clarke cross, and then Fagan latched onto a through ball from Billy McAdams to make it three. City looked to be coasting into the fourth round, and their three-goal lead looked unassailable.

In the second half, the grip City had on the game was nowhere near as strong as it had been, and when Curry was sent sprawling in the penalty area, Casey sent the awarded penalty past Bert Trautmann. City were then denied a strong claim for a penalty when Keith hand-balled. The linesman flagged furiously, but the referee paid no attention.

Fifteen minutes from time, Alex Tait, deputizing for the legendary Jackie Milburn, added yet another touch of excitement to the drama of the closing stages, when he dribbled the ball past three players and scored a great goal with a hard, low shot. With five minutes left, Curry levelled the score for Newcastle, by converting a Davies ball across the face of the goalmouth and into the net, sending the game into extra time.

Then, the scene tense with terrific drama, City went into the lead again. It was Johnstone who got the vital goal, nodding home a McAdams cross. Len White capitalized on a short back pass by Roy Little to Trautmann, and his sharply angled shot flew into the bottom corner.

Newcastle then took the lead for the first time in the game on 105 minutes. It came from a free kick by Casey, and White, only a couple of yards out, chested the ball home. There was still time for Jack Dyson to hit the post with City's last attack.

Newcastle had fought back to snatch a win, defeating City for the first time in ten FA Cup matches, with a tremendous second-half revival. The game more than lived up to its expectations.

Manchester City: Trautmann, Leivers, Little, Barnes, Ewing, Paul, Fagan, McAdams, Johnstone, Dyson, Clarke

Newcastle United: Simpson, Keith, Batty, Scoular, Stokoe, Casey, White, Davies, Tait, Curry, Mitchell

Referee: F.B. Coultas (Hull)

Roy Little recalled, 'At half time we were three up …and Jackie Milburn wasn't playing … so naturally we were pretty confident. His replacement was a guy called Tait, who no-one had heard of, and he hadn't had a kick in the first half. Anyway, in the second half they scored a penalty, then Tait scored, we couldn't believe it!

So, we went into extra time, and early on, Bobby Johnstone scored and we thought we'd got away with it. Then, with a few minutes remaining, they pumped a high ball upfield. I let it go over my head because I had plenty of time, before passing it back to Bert. Anyway, as Bert came out, I underhit the back-pass and White nipped in to toe-poke the ball past him, and then to make matters worse, they scored again. We were stunned, but what a game.'

Season: 1956/57

P	W	D	L	F	A	PTS
42	13	9	20	78	88	35

Division:	One
Position:	Eighteenth
Manager:	Les McDowall
Top Goalscorer:	Bobby Johnstone (19)
Average Attendance:	29,995

West Bromwich Albion v. Manchester City

21 September 1957

Football League First Division
The Hawthorns
Attendance: 25,900

West Bromwich Albion 9
Griffin (3)
Howe (2, inc. pen)
Barlow, Robson, Horobin
Kevan (pen)

Manchester City 2
Clarke, Fagan

Neutral supporters must have loved watching the Blues during this season. Wins, such as 6-2 at home to Everton, were interspersed with defeats, such as 4-8 at Leicester City. Manager Les McDowall tried to evolve some new tactical plans. His first was the dual centre half plan, which, although common in football today, caused chaos among City players and was soon abandoned, after City suffered an embarrassing defeat at The Hawthorns.

An attack of 'flu robbed City of six of their stars, so they were forced to make several changes. City attacked first, Roy Clarke and Billy McAdams joining forces in a rapid attacking move. Joe Hayes then went close with a flying header. Albion hit back, and Whitehouse missed an ideal opportunity to open the scoring on eight minutes: deliberating too long on the ball, he lost possession.

Keith Marsden's presence among the City defenders, made for complete confusion and indecision and, as a result, Albion, aided by an attacking wing half, were able to launch attack after attack. They took a convincing 3-1 lead and had a firm grip on the game by half time. City scrapped their plan and moved to a more orthodox formation, but the Albion outside right, Griffin, was in his element against slack defending. Having scored once in the first half, he waltzed his way through twice more to score himself, and also helped in making two other goals. A goal from Paddy Fagan, early in the second half, enabled City to make the score 3-2. However, within a minute, Albion were two goals ahead, and the massacre there upon took its natural course. It could have been a 14-3 defeat, yet, amazingly enough, there was a suggestion at one stage that Albion might have to make a fight of the game, for City were awarded a penalty while 4-2 down. There was a chance of a come-back, but Ken Barnes missed a spot-kick for the first time since he had been taking them, and the life went out of the City team. The only City player to show a sense of challenge was Dave Ewing, but in his despairing efforts, he conceded two penalties. City were also grateful to stand-in 'keeper John Savage for keeping the score below double figures.

This was Albion's biggest win for more than half a century, but they achieved it against one of the weakest teams seen at The Hawthorns, decimated by injury and illness.

In a remarkable season, City managed to score 104 goals and concede 100, becoming the first team ever to do so. In the reverse fixture, City won 4-1, with goals from McAdams (3) and Colin Barlow.

West Bromwich Albion: Sanders, Howe, Williams, Dudley, Kennedy, Barlow, Griffin, Whitehouse, Robson, Kevan, Horobin

Manchester City: Savage, Branagan, Little, Barnes, Ewing, McTavish, Fagan, Hayes, McAdams, Marsden, Clarke

Referee: N.C. Taylor (Westbury, Wiltshire)

Roy Little recalled, 'We'd leaked a lot of goals prior to this game, and the manager decided we needed to tighten up the defence, so played Keith Marsden, who normally played inside forward, as sweeper, with the back four going man-for-man on their attackers. Unfortunately, Keith wasn't the best reader of a game and, whenever we lost our man, their attackers had a clear run on goal, as Keith wasn't keeping up with play, and we got murdered. Also, it didn't help that big John Savage in goal was not the most agile of 'keepers! It was a complete and utter disaster; needless to say the "Marsden Plan" didn't last very long. After the game, apart from myself, John and Keith were also dropped! Tragically, Keith broke his leg badly in a reserve game again against West Brom a week later, and never played for City again.'

Season: 1957/58

P	W	D	L	F	A	PTS
42	22	5	15	104	100	49

Division:	One
Position:	Fifth
Manager:	Les McDowall
Top Goalscorer:	Joe Hayes (26)
Average Attendance:	32,758

WBA v. Manchester City programme.

LUTON TOWN V. MANCHESTER CITY

28 January 1961

FA Cup Fourth Round
Kenilworth Road, Luton
Attendance: 23,727

Luton Town 2	Manchester City 6
Ashworth (2)	*Law (6)*

Who scored seven goals in a FA Cup tie and ended up on the losing side?

This was the game when Denis Law produced a display of a lifetime to score six goals, only for the referee to abandon the game at Kenilworth Road with the waterlogged pitch unplayable.

On an incredibly wet and muddy pitch, Luton took a two-goal lead in the opening eighteen minutes, Alec Ashworth scoring both goals.

On nineteen minutes, Law scored with a low angle shot, exploiting a gap in the Luton defence and really put City back in the game. Law scored again on thirty-four minutes when Gerry Baker squared inside and Law flung himself forward almost parallel with the ground and headed over the line. He then completed his hat-trick on thirty-seven minutes heading home again from close range.

Within twenty-five minutes of the second half, Law had collected a second hat-trick. His

fourth goal of the game arrived on fifty-one minutes. At the height of a goalmouth struggle, Law nodded post a perplexed goalkeeper. His next goal was the merest of touches, Joe Hayes cracked an angled shot towards the far post and the lively young Scot edged the rebound over the line.

Time was now running out. The players were soaked to the skin and several of the City players had received bumps and bruises as the conditions worsened.

On sixty-seven minutes, Law scored his sixth goal of the game with a drive into the bottom corner of the net. Two minutes later the game was abandoned, the referee deciding that the pitch was now in such a state it was impossible to play football on.

Manager Les McDowell screamed blue murder after failing to persuade the match representatives to continue the

Denis Law spent two periods with City 1960-61 and 1973-74. He played in a total of 80 games and scored 38 goals.

game for the remaining twenty-one minutes. City captain Ken Barnes even said to the referee 'We've played in far worse', but the official had his own way.

A few days later, Ashworth scored two more for Luton in an afternoon replay game and City were beaten 3-1 with Denis Law scoring City's one goal. This gave Law a total of seven goals from the fixture but still meant ending up on the losing side. So, a run-of-the-mill FA Cup tie turned into a match that, decades later, is still the subject of many a trivial pursuit questions and Denis Law was left contemplating that his amazing performance was to no avail.

Luton Town:
Standen, McNally, Bramwell, Pacey, Groves, McGuffie, Noake, Ashworth, Turner, Brown, Fleming

Manchester City:
Trautmann, Leivers, Betts, Barnes, Plenderleith, Shawcross, Barlow, Hannah, Baker, Law, Hayes

Referee: K.R. Tuck (Chesterfield)

Allan Brown, a Luton player, said 'Well you are too good for us, you will easy do it in the replay.'

Season: 1960/61

P	W	D	L	F	A	PTS
42	13	11	18	79	90	37

Division:	One
Position:	Thirteenth
Manager:	Les McDowall
Top Goalscorer:	Denis Law (29)
Average Attendance:	29,407

Manchester City v. Tottenham Hotspur

3 March 1962

Football League First Division
Maine Road, Manchester
Attendance: 31,706

Manchester City 6   Tottenham Hotspur 2
Dobing (3)   *Greaves (2)*
Hayes, Young
Baker (og)

Leslie McDowall put faith in his minors when they faced defending double-winners Tottenham Hotspur and included in his line up John Benson (aged nineteen), Alan Oakes (nineteen), Neil Young (seventeen) and David Wagstaffe (eighteen). City's performances had been improving of late and this tremendous triumph was a morale booster in their fight against relegation.

On the day of the game, the ground was on the heavy side under a covering of more than an inch of snow, some of which was swept onto the running track to allow the pitch to be marked out. The start to the game emphasized the treacherous state of the pitch, as players slithered and fell to the ground.

The Tottenham defence stood firm against a wave of several City attacks and not until the thirteenth minute did Joe Hayes open the scoring for City. Two minutes later, Peter Dobing started a move at the halfway line and ended it with a fine goal after Bobby Kennedy and Colin Barlow, with smart passes, had carried the ball on for him.

The game virtually became a walkover. The entire team clicked, moved confidently and efficiently and left Spurs with hardly a chance. What followed was an incredible half-hour of football that had Spurs fans thinking that the onslaught would possibly inflict upon their team with their

Manchester City team, 1961/62.

heaviest defeat for a number of years.

Dobing scored a further goal for City on forty-seven minutes with a shot that was deflected by Dave Mackay. Neil Young then scored a brilliant individual goal on forty-four minutes, when he brought the ball from the halfway line and beat three men on his way towards the goal before shooting. Barlow was then denied a goal on fifty-two minutes, when all his determination came to no avail as Baker put the ball in his own net. Dobing completed his hat trick on fifty-seven minutes when he fired home a Hayes cross; in truth; he should have had six.

Tottenham then rallied and, fortunately for their morale, Jimmy Greaves, back in favour with the England selectors, and playing in his favoured position of inside left, finally broke the shackles of Benson who had subdued him for most of the game and scored twice.

The score at full time was barely conceivable and the winning margin should have been greater. It could have been 10-2, but as it was, the final score tasted so sweet to City fans that had been waiting for such a result for a long time.

Manchester City: Trautmann, Kennedy, Sear, Benson, Leivers, Oakes, Young, Dobing, Barlow, Hayes, Wagstaffe

Tottenham Hotspur: Hollowbread, Baker, Henry, Blanchflower, Norman, Mackay, Medwin, White, Smith, Greaves, Jones

Referee: G.W. Grundy (Grimsby)

City chairman Alan Douglas commented, 'I think the great victory over Spurs proved we have been right in refusing to be rushed into the transfer market. We could have spent a fortune, but what is satisfying is that most of the youngsters were trained and groomed by us at Maine Road.'

Season: 1961/62

P	W	D	L	F	A	PTS
42	17	7	18	78	81	41

Division:	One
Position:	Twelfth
Manager:	Les McDowall
Top Goalscorer:	Peter Dobing (22)
Average Attendance:	25,626

Manchester City v. Swindon Town

16 January 1965

Football League Second Division
Maine Road, Manchester
Attendance: 8,015

Manchester City 1	Swindon Town 2
Oakes	*Brown*
	Summerbee

The attendances for City's games throughout the early 1960s were slipping, as optimistic City supporters began to vote with their feet when their team failed to give them much satisfaction. In this particular season, City's trademark inconsistency reared its head and games that should have been won ended in defeat. When they were defeated by Shrewsbury Town in the FA Cup, things reached a new low point in the history of the club. Three days later, The Blues were at home to Swindon Town and the attendance was the lowest ever for a League match at Maine Road.

City were hoping for better things after the disasters of the cup, but slumped to their fifth home defeat of the season as Swindon adopted smash-and-grab tactics to seal the points. City outplayed Swindon for the first fifteen minutes and in the opening burst they might have scored several times, but for the splendid keeping of Hicks. A long swerving drive from Cliff Sear was well saved, a header from Trevor Ogden was smartly gathered and attempts by Glyn Pardoe and Derek Kevan went narrowly wide.

Swindon then broke away, and City went behind to a nineteenth-minute goal from Dennis Brown. Rogers crossed from the right flank, and with no one marking Brown, he easily beat Harry Dowd. City still continued to dominate the play: Jimmy Murray hit the cross bar, Dave Bacuzzi shot over, and so did Bobby Kennedy. Two more shots came from Kennedy, one rasping the bar, but for all the pressure City applied there was no tangible reward.

The second half followed pretty much the same pattern and in the sixty-third minute Swindon, in one of their rare attacks, went further ahead. Future Blue, Mike Summerbee, away on the right gathered a pass from Brown, raced into the box and scored a fine goal. Within minutes, City reduced the arrears, Alan Oakes managed to beat Hicks with a shot from thirty yards but, in spite of this overdue success, City's display became more and more ragged.

The match ended in defeat for City and afterwards their supporters expressed their anger. Bricks were hurled at windows in the Main stand, with fans claiming they had suffered enough.

Manchester City: Dowd, Bacuzzi, Sear, Kennedy, Gratrix, Oakes, Pardoe, Murray, Ogden, Kevan, Connor

Swindon Town: Hicks, Dawson, Trollope, Morgan, McPherson, Atherton, Shergold, Hunt, Summerbee, Brown, Rogers

Referee: J.E. Carr (Sheffield)

Manager George Poyser gave his pledge to boost sagging morale, and said 'The club will be going into the transfer market later this week'. He also talked about his absence from the game and a possible scouting trip to check on the form of Johnny Crossan: 'I have not been in touch with the Roker club'.

Season: 1964/65

P	W	D	L	F	A	PTS
42	16	9	17	63	62	41

Division:	Two
Position:	Eleventh
Manager:	George Poyser
Top Goalscorer:	Derek Kevan (20)
Average Attendance:	14,753

Alan Oakes joined the club as an amateur in April 1958 and during eighteen seasons gave incredible service; although there may have been more flamboyant stars around, none were as consistent or as devoted. Oakes started out in a poor City side but went on to play his part in all the club's major honours of the 1960s and '70s. During his City career Alan won First and Second Division Championship medals, an FA Cup, a European Cup Winners Cup and two League Cup medals. Top of the all-time appearances list, Alan played a total of 676 (4) games, scoring 34 goals.

CHARLTON ATHLETIC V. MANCHESTER CITY

13 May 1966

Football League Second Division
The Valley
Attendance: 13,687

Charlton Athletic 2   Manchester City 3
Kenning (pen)   *Oakes*
Saunders   *Connor*
                             Crossan

The season heralded the arrival of two men at the club at a time when it was in its worst ever state. The partnership of Joe Mercer and Malcolm Allison was one that helped guarantee that the Blues would be rediscovered. City's progress continued throughout the season, and they reached the top of the division by October. Mercer's steadying influence and Allison's training methods had brought new life to the club. The Blues were soon marked out as promotion certainties. Colin Bell was bought from Bury and promotion was secured at Rotherham, with a goal from the new signing. The championship was secured nine days later at Charlton.

The pitch was so short of grass as to be almost bald, and both sides found it extremely difficult to control the ball. City, however, showed a readier appreciation of, and a quicker adaptability to, the conditions and Alan Oakes gave them the lead on eighteen minutes. The scoreline remained the same until the half-time interval. City continued to dominate proceedings after the interval and Dave Connor scored a second goal in the forty-ninth minute. When Johnny Crossan accepted a Mike Summerbee pass to make it 3-0, City were coasting with half an hour to go.

First Division-bound City then beat an undignified retreat, when Charlton hit back.

Suddenly, City were reduced to something near panic. Harry Dowd was forced to make several fine saves, and on other occasions, Charlton went very close to scoring. Right-winger Mike Kenning reduced the arrears on sixty-four minutes with a penalty, after Glyn Pardoe was harshly ruled to have fouled Halom. A non-stop blitz from Charlton produced another goal from a future Blues manager, Ron Saunders. With eleven minutes left, he ran through and scored with a fine shot.

City were flattered by the result, and also very hard-pressed to win the game, but still they were First Division-bound, and crowned champions winning the League by five points from nearest rivals Southampton.

Charlton Athletic: Wright, Whitehouse, Kinsey, Halom, Holton, Burridge, Kenning, Campbell, Saunders, Peacock, Glover

Manchester City: Dowd, Kennedy, Horne, Pardoe, Heslop, Oakes, Summerbee, Bell, Young, Crossan, Connor

Referee: K. Styles (Barnsley)

Season: 1965/66

P	W	D	L	F	A	PTS
42	22	15	5	76	44	59

Division: Two
Position: First
Manager: Joe Mercer
Top Goalscorer: Neil Young (17)
Average Attendance: 27,739

Manchester City FC, 1965/66. From left to right, back row: Mike Summerbee, Neil Young, Cliff Sear, Dave Bacuzzi, Mick Doyle, George Heslop, Alan Oakes. Fourth row: Malcolm Allison (assistant manager), Harry Dowd, Alan Ogley, Dave Ewing (assistant trainer). Third row: Johnny Hart (trainer), Bobby Kennedy, Glyn Pardoe, Peter Blakey (physiotherapist.). Second row: Dave Connor, Johnny Crossan (captain). Front row: Joe Mercer (manager).

Manchester City v. Tottenham Hotspur

9 December 1967

Football League First Division
Maine Road, Manchester
Attendance: 35,792

Manchester City 4   Tottenham Hotspur 1
Coleman, Young   *Greaves*
Bell, Summerbee

City continued to perform well during the season, but one game really caught the attention of the football world. There was a clear chance that a victory in this game would send City to the top of the League. It was a real classic, but at first many doubted the game could go ahead as the pitch was covered in snow. However, the ground staff worked hard to make it playable. City came out twenty minutes before the start to get the feel of the snow-covered surface, as trying to get a grip on the frozen pitch was going to prove a hazard.

In the seventh minute, Tottenham were awarded a free-kick just outside the box. Terry Venables' strike deflected off the wall and fell invitingly at the feet of Jimmy Greaves, and the England marksman slotted the ball into the net, well wide of Ken Mulhearn.

Tottenham's lead was not to last, though, as City tore into the Londoners. With the snow still falling, an almighty goalmouth scramble prevailed in the Spurs penalty box. Both Francis Lee and Mike Summerbee had their efforts cleared in desperation, and when a half-clearance by Alan Mullery fell to Colin Bell, he cracked it home to level the scores. It was just what the Blues deserved, as they mastered the conditions.

It was not until the second period that City took a deserved lead. Neil Young crossed from the left, and Summerbee was first to the ball and sent a brilliant looping header past Pat Jennings.

In the sixty-forth minute, Tony Coleman scored a third. Lee fired in an angled shot from the right, which hit the left post and fell to Coleman, who lashed it home with his left foot.

City continued to push forward and overwhelmed a Spurs side packed with internationals. In one attack, a Coleman shot hit the left-hand post, and Young followed up by hitting the right-hand post. Young made amends for his miss when he made it four. Starting a move, he played the ball into Bell in the box, Jennings rushed off his line and the ball cannoned to Young who scored.

Manager Joe Mercer, after the game, complimented his entire side, saying, 'It was the best performance since I came here'. It was a game that fully confirmed the growing strength of the City side, one of those games that will never be forgotten.

Manchester City: Mulhearn, Book, Pardoe, Doyle, Heslop, Oakes, Lee, Bell, Summerbee, Young, Coleman
Sub: Connor

Tottenham Hotspur: Jennings, Kinnear, Knowles, Mullery, Hoy, Mackay, Saul, Greaves, Gilzean, Venables, Jones
Sub: Bond

Referee: D. Smith (Stonehouse)

Tony Book recalled, 'We started the season playing with a sweeper system, but after half-a-dozen games changed it to 4-4-2, and we really gelled as a team. As far as I was concerned, all I had to do was get the ball to Mike Summerbee in front of me, whom I knew with his great pace would get at defenders and cause problems. On the left, Tony Coleman would work the flank, and in Neil Young we had a brilliant player who we would let go and do his thing. The great thing was we had players like Colin Bell, Mike Doyle, Glynn Pardoe and Francis Lee, who all complemented each other, and that's what made us such a strong side.

Of course we had stars like Summerbee, Lee and Bell, but I always felt the key to the team was the likes of the players who had come through the ranks, players like Mick Doyle, Alan Oakes, Neil Young and Glynn Pardoe. They were the nucleus of the side who were already playing in the team, before the likes of Mike and Colin came in around them when it all gelled together.

Colin Bell was an exceptional talent. Colin from box to box was the best; how he covered the ground was incredible. Although he was a simple player, and straightforward, his running power was phenomenal. One moment he'd be defending, then when we broke you always knew he'd be up supporting the forwards.

Finally you cannot underestimate the importance of Joe Mercer and Malcolm Allison. Joe was the father figure, everyone respected him and looked up to him, and, for me, he was a great PR man. Then there was Malcolm who brought me to the club. He did the coaching and during that era there was no better coach in the country, he was first class and, without a doubt, was twenty years ahead of his time.'

George Heslop signed for City from Everton and played in 198 games between 1965 and 1971, scoring 3 goals.

READING V. MANCHESTER CITY

31 January 1968

FA Cup Third Round Replay
Elm Park, Reading
Attendance: 25,659

Reading 0   Manchester City 7
                 Summerbee (3)
                 Heslop, Bell
                 Young, Coleman

Reading paid dearly for their goal-less draw in the third round of the FA Cup at Maine Road. The Third Division side had packed their defence to earn a replay, but after this game, City had to ask the question of themselves: 'How did they get involved in a replay?'

So often in the Cup, the differences between a leading club and one in the lower divisions vanishes in the urgency and excitement of the competition. However, Reading's life in the FA Cup was cut short by an avalanche – in fact, they were murdered!

It was surprising that City did not go ahead in the game until the twenty-sixth minute. A free-kick from Tony Coleman found the head of George Heslop, and 'keeper Dixon had no chance of stopping Heslop's first ever goal for City. Two minutes later, Mike Summerbee headed the first of the goals that would give him a hat-trick. Neil Young lobbed the ball to the far post, Colin Bell headed it back and Summerbee nodded it past Dixon.

Reading had their only chance to get back into the game just before half time. Allen sent Collins clear, but his shot swung away from the direction of the goal and missed the far post.

Mike Summerbee was Joe Mercer's first signing at Maine Road. Initially an orthodox outside-right, he created havoc for opposing defences with his accurate crossing. Summerbee eventually played a more versatile role and shared in many of the club's successes. A member of the First and Second Division Championship, FA Cup and 1970 League Cup winning sides, Mike is eighth on the all-time appearances list, having played a total of 449 (3) matches, scoring 68 goals. In addition, Mike was capped 8 times by England.

At the start of the second half, Summerbee tapped in City's third, and then Bell struck the fourth goal of the game after sixty-three minutes when he outpaced four men to score emphatically from 20 yards. Coleman then scored the goal of the game after seventy-four minutes. Summerbee fed Francis Lee on the right and his angled pass found Bell. He cut into the middle, then sent the ball between two defenders for Coleman to run onto and ram the ball into the back of the net.

Summerbee grabbed his third in the eightieth minute, after Dixon failed to hold a free-kick, and six minutes from time, Neil Young strode through the middle on his own, lashing home a tremendous 20-yarder, to score City's seventh goal and complete the rout.

Reading never managed to combat the pace of Bell, Young and Summerbee. The seven-goal romp prompted a loudspeaker announcement to tell the capacity-filled Elm Park crowd: 'You have been privileged to see the finest side in the League tonight.'

This was a thoroughly professional performance by City, full of rhythm, blend and just about everything else that demonstrated why they were the most exciting side in football at the time. It also provided manager Joe Mercer with his finest goal feast since taking over the club.

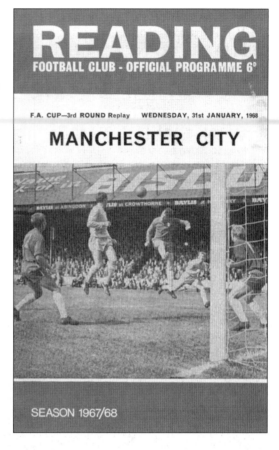

Reading:
Dixon, Bacuzzi, Spiers, Meldrum, Bayliss, Yard, Foster, Allen, Collins, Smee, Harris

Manchester City:
Mulhearn, Book, Pardoe, Doyle, Heslop, Oakes, Lee, Bell, Summerbee, Young, Coleman

Referee: E.T. Jennings (Stourbridge)

Newcastle United v. Manchester City

11 May 1968

Football League First Division
St James Park, Newcastle
Attendance: 46,300

Newcastle United 3
Robson, Sinclair, McNamee

Manchester City 4
Young 2
Summerbee, Lee

Top of the table on goal difference, a victory for the Blues would clinch the First Division Championship for the first time in thirty years. The title had dramatically come down to the last day of the campaign, and the race was between City and fierce local rivals Manchester United. City had a difficult away game at Newcastle, whose home form was exemplary.

A legion of nearly 20,000 City fans in a steady stream of coaches and cars headed up the A1 to St James Park, in order to watch one of the most significant and exciting games in the history of Manchester City.

In a match of tremendously swaying fortunes, City opened nervously. Mike Summerbee grabbed the goal on thirteen minutes that City desperately needed, but within two minutes, Bryan 'Pop' Robson had equalized, and City had to start all over again.

Just after the half-hour mark, a Summerbee throw-in found Colin Bell, who passed inside to Alan Oakes. His initial shot was charged down, but Neil Young restored the lead, crisply hitting a glorious goal. Once again, Newcastle equalized swiftly through Jackie Sinclair. Newcastle then had further chances to score before half-time arrived with both sides level.

The Blues came out for the second half in full cry, refusing to buckle under the tension of the day and, within three minutes, Young put City back in front. It was Francis Lee's turn to get into the action next. He had a goal disallowed before giving City a two-goal cushion, when he ran onto another superb through ball from Bell.

Newcastle were still not going to give up without a fight. Five minutes from time, John McNamee abandoned his centre half role to score a third Newcastle goal. In those nerve-shattering final remaining

Manchester City FC, 1967/68.

Francis Lee securess the title with City's fourth.

minutes, City and their supporters lived on a knife-edge and endured a tense ending as the Magpies chased an equalizer.

It never came and, as the final whistle blew, St James Park was invaded by thousands of joyous City supporters, making the pitch a sea of blue and white. Those who witnessed the football extravaganza will swell with emotion as they reminiscence about the unique atmosphere and non-stop action which saw City clinch the League Championship for the first time since 1937 in the most exciting manner possible.

Ironically, victory was not essential because Sunderland pulled off a shock result at Old Trafford, beating Manchester United 2-1.

Newcastle United: McFaul, Craig, Clark, Moncur, McNamee, Iley, Sinclair, Scott, Davies, B. Robson, T. Robson

Manchester City: Mulhearn, Book, Pardoe, Doyle, Heslop, Oakes, Lee, Bell, Summerbee, Young, Coleman

Referee: R.B. Kirkpatrick (Lewiston)

Within minutes of their title success, Joe Mercer commented: 'We are champions because we deserve to be, because we are very, very fit. There is a lot of team spirit and we have allowed people to express themselves naturally. We work hard, and play positively, and the players – and we must never forget that these are the men who really deserve it – are better than even we realized.'

Malcolm Allison: 'We have had more courage than the majority of teams in the League, the courage to play this game. We work at things and are consistently disciplined. Any side we play at home or away has got to be at their best to beat us.'

Mike Doyle: 'We've played more consistently than anyone else, I think we did it without luck as well. Everyone works for everyone else and there is good team spirit.'

Colin Bell: 'The output of effort is something we are proud of and it is there even in the most desperate situations. The lads never give up, even when they are behind. We are at our best when the pressure is on, and the pressure was on during the last half of the season.'

Neil Young: 'We are the fittest side in the country. We lasted the season better than anyone else and grew in confidence. We murdered sides in the last twenty minutes, when they had given their lot against us. Apart from the short absence of Colin Bell, we have been lucky with injuries, and this has helped. When you lose more than one player, it can affect the pattern of the team's play. The turning point was our win at Old Trafford.'

Alan Oakes: 'We are a great side and we have all worked hard. Most clubs expected us to crack and nobody thought we were capable of winning the title. We're the underdogs who have bitten hard at everybody.'

Tony Coleman: 'The lads worked hard and deserve everything they have got. We play the most attractive football in the First Division when we are allowed to play. The determination in the team is fantastic – this team never knows when it is beaten.'

Glyn Pardoe: 'We have been made to believe in ourselves. We've come out and attacked teams – always going for goal. Everything stems from our training; it's so enjoyable. The boss and Malcolm have given us confidence to do things and, without doubt, the match at Manchester United proved finally to all fair-minded judges that we had a valid claim for the title.'

Vince Wilson, *Sunday Mirror*: 'They were magnificent. A blue lightning-speed outfit refusing to change the mood which spelled only victory. If the ideal championship winner exists at all, then this is it. It was City's Championship. They did it in wonderful style.'

Eric Cooper, *Daily Express*: ' It was this effort by Newcastle, exceeding in skill and efficiency in most of their victories this season, that made the superb merit of City's triumph all the more glorious. In such an atmosphere of fast, open football and fierce tension, mistakes were excusable, but City were never less than Champions.'

Frank McGhee, *Daily Mirror*: 'Even in the final match when tension was almost tangible and caution understandable, Manchester City found the courage and confidence to go forward attacking.'

James Mossop, *Sunday Express*: 'A magnificent show. World champions in every sense. A credit to football. A credit to Joe Mercer.'

Ronald Crowther, *Daily Mail*: 'The important thing about being Champions is to look like Champions. And sure enough, Manchester City strode home past the winning post at Newcastle with all the flair and conviction of footballers for whom this final issue was never in doubt.'

Looking back on the Newcastle match, Tony Book recalled: 'Throughout the game there was a feeling among the team that we were not going to lose. The type of team we were, we were always attacking and going forward so chances would come, but credit to Newcastle they kept on coming back at us, but we were so determined that day; it never looked as if we would lose the game. However, what I remember most about the day was the journey home. There were thousands and thousands of fans

Francis Lee signed for City from Bolton Wanderers, played in 328 games between 1967-1974. He scored 148 goals.

following the coach home; it was absolutely incredible. We wanted to stop for a celebratory drink but because of the following we couldn't, and when we got back to Manchester the scenes were indescribable.'

Season: 1967/68

P	W	D	L	F	A	PTS
42	26	6	10	86	43	58

Division: One
Position: First
Manager: Joe Mercer
Top Goalscorer: Neil Young (21)
Average Attendance: 37,206

Programme from the game.

MANCHESTER CITY V. FENERBAHCE S.K.

18 September 1968

European Cup, Round One
Maine Road, Manchester
Attendance: 38,787

Manchester City 0   Fenerbahce S.K. 0

This was City's first ever game in a European competition, and they faced the champions of Turkey in what was the first ever competitive European Cup meeting between an English side and a Turkish side.

City's game plan was simple, aiming for a two-goal lead to take into the return leg. That could have come about after the opening twenty minutes of the game, when the Blues had several clear-cut scoring chances. Francis Lee and Mike Summerbee both fired low shots just inches wide of the post, and Simsek Yavuz, a Turkish u-23 international, somehow blocked a blistering drive from Colin Bell on his line. It was during this spell that the Turks were at their most vulnerable, as City showed the better, more cohesive football, but they were up against a team who played to a strict game plan.

Yavuz rescued his side again just before the half-time interval. Mike Doyle had lashed in an accurate and powerful shot, which the 'keeper had not seen but somehow managed to turn the ball out for a corner. The pressure continued in the second half, as Ercan cleared a Bell header off the line. Despite City commanding virtually all the play, they still could not break down a well-organized Fenerbahce defence who were defending their proud record of only having conceded 12 goals in 34 games.

When the Turks did attack, from time to time, in an attempt to try and take a lead back to Istanbul, City panicked. A through ball by Nedim gave Abdullah a scoring chance, but his shot was blocked. Substitute Fuat also tested Ken Mulhearn with a difficult lob.

Thousands of disgruntled City fans streamed out of the ground more than ten minutes before the end of the game, frustrated by their team's inability to finish any of the many chances they had created. It was to be one of those nights that, no matter how long the game lasted, there was no way City were going to score. Credit must be given to a controlled and measured performance by the

From left to right, back row: Oakes, Young, Heslop, Mulhearn, Bell, Pardoe, Summerbee. Front row: Allison (assistant manager), Connor, Lee, Book, Colman, Doyle, Hart (trainer).

Players boarding the plane before the flight to Istanbul for the first leg.

Turks. At the end, 'keeper Yavuz was chaired off to tremendous ovation, such was the part he had played in the game.

The return leg a fortnight later saw City take an early lead through a goal by Tony Coleman, but Fenerbahce scored twice to win the tie. City had fallen at their first European hurdle.

Manchester City:
Mulhearn, Kennedy, Pardoe, Doyle, Heslop, Oakes, Lee, Bell, Summerbee, Young, Coleman

Fenerbahce:
Yavuz, Sukru, Levent, Ercan, Nunweiller, Selim, Ziya, Yilmaz, Abdullah, Nedim, Can
Sub: Fuat

Referee: L. Van Ravens (Holland)

Colin Bell commented: 'It was unfortunate that it was our first experience of Europe, and it couldn't have been a bigger tournament. They kicked us up in the air, picked us up, shook our hands and we accepted it'.

Manchester City v. Burnley

7 December 1968

Football League First Division
Maine Road, Manchester
7 December 1968
Attendance: 31,009

Manchester City 7   Burnley 0
Bell (2), Young (2)
Doyle, Lee, Coleman

City's entertaining style of football had helped create many admirers, so much so that they had to designate certain seating areas purely for season ticket holders. In fact, such was the increase in their popularity that they had to make admittance to the main stand by ticket only.

Inconsistency seemed to dominate the Blues' League performances, and one game that typified everything was against Burnley. City scored seven, missed a penalty, were foiled at least three times by brilliant goalkeeping and for nearly twenty minutes played with only ten men.

City were looking for goals right from the start of the match and within two minutes their persistence paid off. As a reward for some quick thinking and astute passing, Neil Young was the last player to receive the ball and he took his goal well. Young scored a second on twenty-seven minutes and surely must have taken the eye of the watching England manager, Sir Alf Ramsey. Colin Bell, City's inside forward, also turned on his immense talents for the benefit of Ramsey, and scored the Blues' third goal on thirty-nine minutes.

City missed their penalty early in the second half, which had been awarded when Jones

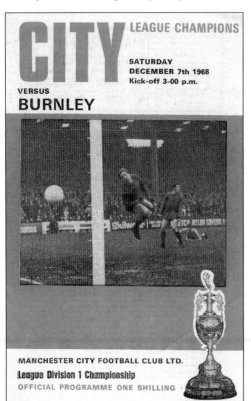

fouled Francis Lee. Lee took the penalty, which ended with him driving the ball in the direction of the corner flag. So in control of the game were City that certain Burnley players were becoming frustrated with their lack of success on the pitch and resorted to constant hacking and kicking of their superior opponents. Two players, Latcham and Blant, were booked for committing fouls out of sheer exasperation.

Tony Coleman bounced back into the City attack after missing two matches following tough disciplinary action at boardroom level after a night club incident with assistant manager, Malcolm Allison, and marked his return by scoring in the fifty-first minute.

There was little from Burnley to extend the City defence, and only once did they look like scoring. After a bad pass back by Glyn Pardoe, Casper nipped in and shot, but Tommy Booth kicked the ball off the line. The nightmare afternoon for Burnley was concluded when Mike Doyle scored on sixty-five minutes. Bell scored his second in the final minutes, his performance having brought two goals, and he made four others. Burnley's youthful side had been brushed aside. City had exposed the weakness of the opposition to indulge in a carefree, remorseless display of attacking football. City did all this with the ease and superb confidence of a team that later went on to win the FA Cup. City had achieved their highest League score for five years and attained what turned out to be the biggest League win under the Mercer/Allison reign.

Manchester City: Dowd, Pardoe, Mann, Doyle, Booth, Oakes, Lee, Bell, Summerbee, Young, Coleman
Sub: Connor

Burnley: Jones, Smith, Latcham, O'Neil, Wrigley, Blant, Thomas, Bellamy, Dobson, Casper, Kindon
Sub: Collins

Referee: D. Lyden (Birmingham)

Season: 1968/69

P	W	D	L	F	A	PTS
42	15	10	17	64	55	40

Division:	One
Position:	Thirteenth
Manager:	Joe Mercer
Top Goalscorer:	Francis Lee (18)
Average Attendance:	33,715

Mike Doyle was one of the club's greatest players during the Mercer/Allison era. Starting out as a centre forward he made his name as a determined midfielder or defender, who was eventually appointed club captain. Mick won 5 caps for England and, apart from Alan Oakes, is the only City player to win the First and Second Division Championship, FA Cup, two League Cup, and European Cup Winners Cup winners medals. Third on the all-time appearances list, Mick played in 563 (7) matches, scoring 41 goals.

97

LEICESTER CITY V. MANCHESTER CITY

26 April 1969

FA Cup final
Wembley, London
Attendance 100,000

Leicester City 0   Manchester City 1
                          Young

The last time City had been at Wembley in a FA Cup Final was thirteen years ago in the memorable match against Birmingham City.

This time, their opponents were a team struggling to avoid relegation from the Second Division, Leicester City. Leicester were no strangers to City in the FA Cup, both teams had met each other for the last three successive seasons in the competition.

City were at full strength and lay claim to a forward line of match winners, such as Mike Summerbee, Colin Bell, Francis Lee and Neil Young. City were, therefore, strong favourites, and were expected to overwhelm Leicester.

Malcolm Allison was forced to watch the game from a seat in the stands as he was serving a touchline ban, so his place was taken on the bench by the City mascot, who, incidentally, was the first ever in a Wembley Cup Final.

Leicester's record signing Allan Clarke, a £150,000 purchase from Fulham, forced Harry Dowd to make a fine save in the opening exchanges. This signalled the beginning of some fine attacking play from both sides. City were forced to work hard against an active Leicester side, full of beans, who refused to be intimidated by the occasion.

Twenty-three minutes into the match, Lee took a throw-in which reached Summerbee. He went past David Nish and Woolett, cut the ball back from the dead ball line, and Young ran to meet the cross, hitting it with the outside of his left foot past Peter Shilton's right hand and into the roof of the net.

It proved to be the only goal of the game, although Leicester did have their chances. Full-back Rodrigues came close, and Clarke had a long range shot before setting up an ideal opportunity for Lochhead to score, when he headed down a Glover cross, but the centre forward mishit his volley over the bar from a good position.

City dug deep into their resources, banking on their perseverance and skill to preserve their supremacy. They clung on enough, and had sufficient in reserve to hold out until the final whistle to add another trophy to their cabinet.

Leicester, to their credit, played their part in an entertaining and honourable game, but it was to be Tony Book who climbed the steps to the royal box and collected the FA Cup from Princess Anne.

It was after this famous victory that a little City tale came to light, when an example of the eccentric behaviour of a starry-eyed Tony Coleman was highlighted. When being presented to Princess Anne prior to the kick-off, he had been at a loss what to say and was to be overheard saying, 'Give my regards to your mum

FOOTBALL ASSOCIATION CHALLENGE CUP COMPETITION

FINAL

Leicester City
v
Manchester City

SATURDAY 26th APRIL 1969 · Kick-Off 3 p.m.

EMPIRE STADIUM WEMBLEY Official Programme 2/-

From left to right, back row: Blakey (physiotherapist), Pardoe, Doyle, Oakes, Dowd, Bell, Booth, Ewing (trainer). Front row: Owen, Connor, Summerbee, Book (captain), Lee, Young, Coleman.

and dad', much to the astonishment and entertainment of his colleagues.

Leicester City: Shilton, Rodrigues, Nish, Roberts, Woolett, Cross, Fern, Gibson, Lochhead, Clarke, Glover (Manley)

Manchester City: Dowd, Book, Pardoe, Doyle, Booth, Oakes, Summerbee, Bell, Lee, Young, Coleman
Sub: Connor

Referee: G. McCabe (Sheffield)

Joe Mercer commented after the triumph, 'We were determined to play attractive football and before the boys went out, they were told to give the public a display they'd remember. I think they succeeded.'

Neil Young, the scorer, said of his winning strike, 'In these situations you don't have time to aim for a particular spot. You just sense the chance, hit it, and hope for the best. I thought I did everything right with my first chance, but it went over and the same could have happened when I scored.'

Tony Book recalled, 'I missed the early part of the season and one of my first games back was against Newcastle, who we beat 2-0 in the replay. The final was my first match at Wembley and I have so many memories of the day, but one that stands out was when Tony Coleman told Princess Anne, "Give my regards to your mum and dad" when I was introducing the team during the pre-match formalities. What a character he was. As for the match, Leicester weren't playing particularly well so we were confident but, to be fair to them, they did make it difficult for us. As for what I remember most, that would be Mike Summerbee's pull-back for Neil Young to strike the goal. They say that Wembley takes it out of you, but even though I was thirty-odd years old, I had enough energy to receive the Cup!'

Manchester City v. Manchester United

15 November 1969

Football League First Division
Maine Road, Manchester
Attendance: 63,013

Manchester City 4   Manchester United 0
Bell (2)
Sadler (og)
Young

This was the season when both the Manchester sides met each other on no less than five occasions. The League Cup saw both sides drawn against each other at the two-legged semi-final stage, and, for the second time in the history of the derby, City upset United's Wembley aspirations at the last but one hurdle. City had won the first leg in dramatic style at Maine Road 2-1, and the second leg was as equally breathtaking, in front of an excited and expectant capacity crowd. An Alex Stepney mistake allowed Mike Summerbee to equalize on the night and send City through to the final as aggregate winners. United then gained sweet revenge for the defeat in the League Cup by dumping City, who were the reigning holders, out of the FA Cup, to restore some pride.

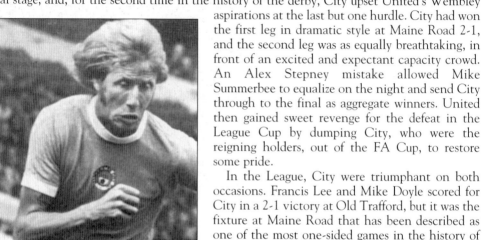

In the League, City were triumphant on both occasions. Francis Lee and Mike Doyle scored for City in a 2-1 victory at Old Trafford, but it was the fixture at Maine Road that has been described as one of the most one-sided games in the history of derby football.

United almost took the lead in the first minute but Denis Law's outstretched foot missed an opportunity presented to him by John Aston. That was to be United's one and only real goal-scoring chance and they then spent the rest of the game ineffectively trying to hold off surge after surge of City attacks.

Not until thirty-eight minutes had been played did the first breakthrough arrive, when Neil Young arched a shot past Alex Stepney to give the Blues the lead at the half-time break.

City continued to dictate the pattern of the game, and early in the second half, Colin Bell drove the ball into the net. It was at this point that the resistance of United's defenders, such as David Sadler and Francis Burns, wilted. In a desperate effort to clear the ball under pressure, Sadler turned a cross past Stepney to give City a third goal.

Colin Bell signed for City from Bury and played in 498 games between 1966-1979, scoring 153 goals.

The superior fitness and confidence of the City players forced their rivals to capitulate, and the rout was completed in the last minute, when Colin Bell arrived at the far post to slide the ball over the line.

This was quite simply a one-sided game and the impressive teamwork of City simply outclassed United in every department. They had complete supremacy and left the pitch to a standing ovation.

Manchester City: Corrigan, Book, Pardoe, Doyle, Booth, Oakes, Summerbee, Bell, Lee, Young, Bowyer
Sub: Connor

Manchester United: Stepney, Brennan, Dunne, Burns, Ure, Sadler, Sartori, (Kidd), Best, Charlton, Law. Aston

Referee: G.W. Hill (Leicester)

Tony Book: 'Derby games were always special, there was always a full house and the atmosphere was electric. The atmosphere leading up to a derby was always fantastic, fans were always clamouring for tickets and you could never get enough to please everyone. Occasionally, derby games never lived up to expectations, but some of them were brilliant, and this was no exception, especially scoring four against them. I loved playing in them, they were always very competitive and great occasions.'

Season: 1969/70

P	W	D	L	F	A	PTS
42	16	11	15	55	48	43

Division: One
Position: Tenth
Manager: Joe Mercer
Top Goalscorer: Francis Lee (22)
Average Attendance: 33,940

MANCHESTER CITY V. WEST BROMWICH ALBION

7 March 1970

Football League Cup Final
Wembley Stadium, London
Attendance: 97,963

Manchester City 2   West Bromwich Albion 1
Doyle   *Astle*
Pardoe

City reached the final of the League Cup in 1970 and the significance of this was it was the first time they had ever done so in this particular competition. There were also a couple of other unique facts about this competition: City were the first team to bring the League Cup back to Lancashire, and it was also the first season that all ninety-two league clubs had taken part.

City did not have the best of preparations for what, at the time, was still considered to be a prestigious competition. In the week before the final, City had flown out to Portugal to play Academica Coimbra in a European Cup Winners cup fixture and when they returned to England, they heard the news that the staging of the Horse of the Year event had ruined the Wembley pitch.

Current City reserve team coach Asa Hartford had a hand in the first goal of the game. His through-ball to Albion's England striker, Jeff Astle, saw big Joe Corrigan turn the resulting shot past the post for a corner. From the corner, a half-clearance to the wing was hoisted back in and Astle was the first to be alert, heading home to give West Brom the lead after only six minutes. This gave City the impetus to forge ahead with an all-out assault, but it looked as though it was going to be one of those days. No matter what City did the equalizer looked as if it would never come.

Then, on sixty-five minutes, a Glyn Pardoe corner was flicked on and a first-time shot from Mike Doyle brought City level.

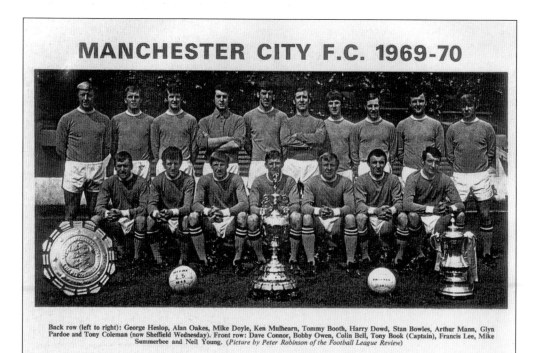

MANCHESTER CITY F.C. 1969-70

Back row (left to right): George Heslop, Alan Oakes, Mike Doyle, Ken Mulhearn, Tommy Booth, Harry Dowd, Stan Bowles, Arthur Mann, Glyn Pardoe and Tony Coleman (now Sheffield Wednesday). Front row: Dave Connor, Bobby Owen, Colin Bell, Tony Book (Captain), Francis Lee, Mike Summerbee and Neil Young. (*Picture by Peter Robinson of the Football League Review*)

The inspirational Mike Summerbee then had to leave the field of play with a hairline fracture of the left leg and, although Francis Lee almost stole the match near the end, City were forced to play an extra thirty minutes on what by then was a terrible surface.

The question on everybody's lips was whether City were capable of another gruelling thirty minutes on such a surface, especially after the hard-fought European tie and the previous ninety minutes of action. Although tired from the effects of two difficult games, City's superior fitness showed and Albion could not compete. After 112 minutes, Glyn Pardoe hooked home a Colin Bell back-header for his first goal of the season and, more importantly, to give City the lead, one that Albion could not reduce and City won the trophy.

This was another fine victory for Manchester City in their now famous red-and-black stripes and, despite conceding an early goal, they fought their way back to a thrilling victory in extra time.

Manchester City: Corrigan, Book, Mann, Doyle, Booth, Oakes, Heslop, Bell, Summerbee (Bowyer), Lee, Pardoe

West Brom: Osborne, Fraser, Wilson, Brown, Talbot, Kaye, Cantello, Suggett, Astle, Hartford (Krzywicki), Hope

Referee: V. James (York)

After the match, Joe Mercer was delighted: 'What a magnificent side. I was worried when Albion went ahead because Joe Corrigan should have got that ball, but we made up for it afterwards, and as for Tony Book, what a great captain … what a great man. All the players – all twenty-four of them – showed that the British professional is the best in the world.'

Francis Lee was undoubtedly man of the match: 'Everything I tried came off, that's why I told Malcolm before extra time to tell the lads to let me have as much of the ball as they could'.

Glyn Pardoe added, 'I didn't mind the mud, but some of the lads were shattered. But what a time to get your first goal of the season'.

Tony Book: 'We had a hard match against Academia in Portugal a few days earlier, drawing 0-0, and it was snowing when we came back so we were delayed. Eventually, we landed at Birmingham so the build-up for that particular game was not particularly good and, to compound matters, the state of the ground was appalling. Although we were odds on to win, we got off to a bad start and went a goal down early on, but Mike Doyle and Glyn Pardoe grabbed goals for us for a great win. What I also remember was Francis Lee's performance in this final, which summed up for me what he was all about. We weren't playing well, and at extra time I'll always remember him saying, 'get the ball to me and I'll do the rest,' and he did. He had a tremendous confidence in his own ability and was great to have in your side. Looking back, I'd won everything domestically in a really short period of time, which was just amazing'.

Manchester City v. Gornik Zabrze

29 April 1970

European Cup Winners Cup Final
Prater Stadium
Attendance: 10,000

Manchester City 2   Gornik Zabrze 1
Young, Lee (pen)   *Ozlizlo*

A special place in Manchester City's hall of fame must belong to the team and the occasion that produced the club's only European final victory.

The Blues were in a confident mood and not even the sparse crowd and terrible weather conditions would prevent this from being a night of glory for City.

At least 4,000 Blues supporters were in the crowd, but there were very few Polish supporters due to travelling restrictions.

Those loyal fans were not to be disappointed, despite being drenched through by torrential and persistent rain. Their spirits were raised in the twefth minute when City went ahead. Francis Lee out on the left wing cut inside and his shot proved to be to blistering for the goalkeeper. As it skidded along the wet surface, Kostka could only parry it to Neil Young, who followed up and put the loose ball away.

City then lost Mike Doyle with an injured ankle, following a clash midway through the first half. The Blues, however, did not let this setback be in any way a detriment to their main aim, and they continued to push forward. Three minutes before half-time, Young broke free down the middle, took the ball around Kostka, only to be brought down by the despairing 'keeper.

The above programme was given away free at the game. But can you spot the difference?

104

Die bisherigen Europacup-Pokalsieger

1961	FC FLORENZ	1965	WESTHAM-LONDON
1962	ATLETICO-MADRID	1966	BORUSSIA-DORTMUND
1963	TOTTENHAM-HOTSPUR	1967	FC BAYERN-MÜNCHEN
1964	SPORTING-LISSABON	1968	AC MILAN
	1969	SLOVAN-BRATISLAVA	

Europacup der Pokalsieger 1969/70

QUALIFIKATION

Rapid-Wien – Torpedo-Moskau	0 : 0	1 : 1

ERSTE HAUPTRUNDE

Mjoendalen IF – **Cardiff City**	1 : 7	1 : 5
FC Magdeburg – MTK Budapest	1 : 0	1 : 1
Dukla-Prag – **Olympique-Marseille**	1 : 0	0 : 2
Glasgow Rangers – Steaua-Bukarest	2 : 0	0 : 0
Dinamo-Zagreb – Slovan-Bratislava	3 : 0	0 : 0
IFK Norrköping – Sliema-Wanderers	5 : 1	0 : 1
Göztöpe-Izmir – US Luxemburg	3 : 0	3 : 2
Rapid-Wien – **PSV Eindhoven**	1 : 2	2 : 4
Ards – **AS Roma**	0 : 0	1 : 3
Lierse SK – Apoel-Nikosia	10 : 1	1 : 0
Frem-Kopenhagen – Sankt Gallen	2 : 1	0 : 1
Olympiakos-Piräus – **Gornik-Zabrze**	2 : 2	0 : 5
Academica-Coimbra – Kuopio-Palloseura	0 : 0	1 : 0
Atletico-Bilbao – **Manchester City**	3 : 3	0 : 3
Shamrock Rovers – **FC Schalke 04**	2 : 1	0 : 3
Valstman-Reykjavik – **Levsky-Sofia**	0 : 4	0 : 4

ACHTELFINALE

Olympique-Marseille – **Dinamo-Zagreb**	1 : 1	0 : 2
IFK Norrköping – **FC Schalke 04**	0 : 0	0 : 1
Gornik-Zabrze – Glasgow Rangers	3 : 1	3 : 1
AS Roma – PSV Eindhoven	1 : 0	0 : 1
Göztöpe-Izmir – Cardiff-City	3 : 0	0 : 1
FC Magdeburg – **Academica-Coimbra**	1 : 0	0 : 2
Lierse SK – **Manchester City**	0 : 3	0 : 5
Levsky-Sofia – Sankt Gallen	4 : 0	0 : 0

VIERTELFINALE

AS Roma – Göztöpe-Izmir	2 : 0	0 : 0
Gornik-Zabrze – Levsky-Sofia	2 : 1	2 : 3
FC Schalke 04 – Dinamo-Zagreb	3 : 1	1 : 0
Manchester City – Academica-Coimbra	1 : 0	0 : 0

SEMIFINALE

FC Schalke 04 – **Manchester City**		1 : 0	1 : 5
AS Roma – **Gornik-Zabrze**	1 : 1	2 : 2	1 : 1

FINALE

Manchester-City – Gornik-Zabrze

The route to the final.

Lee stepped up and converted the resulting penalty, which he shot straight at Kostka, the ball going through the goalkeeper's legs.

In the second half, Gornik, with nothing to lose, exerted some pressure and a fraught ending to the game was guaranteed after Ozlizlo scored on sixty-eight minutes. A free-kick taken by Szoltysik found Lubanski, who in turn passed to his captain to pull back a goal. It looked as though City might face a late fight-back from the crack Polish team.

Despite one or two anxious moments, the Blues stayed solid and could have scored again near the end, but substitute Ian Bowyer missed a splendid chance. All was worthwhile when the final whistle was blown with the score at 2-1, and Tony Book was soon holding aloft the third major trophy City had won in twelve months.

It may have been pouring down with rain on the night, but the morale was not left dampened. The men in blue triumphed over adversity to secure one of the most coveted prizes in football. This was a final that will live in the memory of every City fan who witnessed the match and the emotion of victory.

By beating Gornik, Manchester City became the first English team to win all three domestic competitions (First Division Championship, FA Cup and League Cup) and a European trophy.

Manchester City: Corrigan, Book, Pardoe, Doyle (Bowyer), Booth, Oakes, Heslop, Lee, Young, Bell, Towers

Gornik Zabrze: Kostka, Latocha, Ozlizlo, Gorgan, Forenski (Deja), Szoltysik, Wilczek (Skowrone), Olek, Banas, Lubanski, Szarynbiski

Referee: P. Schiller (Austria)

Prior to the final, Mercer commented, 'The last time we played in Europe we failed miserably, going out to Fenerbahce. We were overconfident. But we haven't made that mistake this season and we can win this cup.' After the game, he said, 'My team had orders to attack whenever there was a chance. It paid off ... Defences must be driven into the ground with the utmost individual determination when chances come ... That's why I like to see brave wingers stretch defences until they suddenly snap in the middle. With this victory, the lads really proved that they are the greatest.'

Tony Book: 'Of the run, the away tie against Bilbao was by far the toughest, and I remember we recovered from two goals down to draw 3-3, before winning comfortably at home in the return. Also, we just scraped past Academia with a last-minute goal in extra time of the second leg in the quarters through Tony Towers. However, what sticks in my memory about this final was it had been a beautiful day all day, so I thought this will be great tonight, then the heavens opened. The attendance was not great, but the supporters there that night really cheered us through. They were wonderful times for the club.'

Opposite page. Top: Neil Young bundles home City's opening goal on a rain-soaked evening in Vienna, where a crowd of just 10,000 witnessed the club's greatest European night as Gornik Zabrze were defeated 2-1. Bottom: Tony Book raises his fourth trophy in three seasons. City now had the honour of becoming the first English side to win a European competition and all three domestic trophies.

MANCHESTER CITY V. WOLVERHAMPTON WANDERERS

2 March 1974

Football League Cup Final
Wembley Stadium, London
Attendance: 100,000

Manchester City 1	Wolverhampton Wanderers 2
Bell	*Hibbitt, Richards*

Many of the City players who appeared in this game felt the game had been lost before they even went onto the Wembley pitch. They explained that they were not in the right frame of mind to go out and play to the best of their abilities, claiming they had been treated like children by manager Ron Saunders in the team hideaway in the build-up to the match.

City fielded five international forwards and were considered to be favourites to win the game. Throughout the first half, City were the more powerful side but, very much against the run of play, Wolves took the lead on forty-three minutes. Kenny Hibbitt's partly mishit drive beat City 'keeper Keith Macrae and crept in at the far post to give Wolves a 1-0 half-time lead.

In the second half, City went forward looking for an equalizer and a few opportunities came the Blues' way. Palmer deflected an effort from Tommy Booth off the line and a header from Francis Lee went over the bar. On sixty minutes, City got themselves back into the game when Rodney Marsh tormented Wolves' left flank and centred for Colin Bell to fire home an equalizer.

It was no wonder that Wolves manager Bill McGarry ran straight to his goalkeeper, Pierce, at the final whistle, because he, more than anyone, helped Wolves to their first major trophy in a number of years. Pierce was forced to make brilliant saves from Marsh, Lee and Bell as The Blues tore into Wolves. If the game had been a boxing match, the opposition would have thrown in the towel. After City had got the scores level, they were never out of the Wolves half. Bell saw a shot hit the underside of the bar but, once again, luck eluded City.

Then, totally against the run of play, Sunderland ran to the goal line and pulled the ball back across the area, Marsh just got a toe to it and helped it in the direction of John Richards, who scored an eighty-fifth minute winner. Everyone connected with the Blues was saddened by the scoreline, in particular, Marsh, who refused to collect his losers' tankard, blaming himself for the defeat.

Wolverhampton Wanderers: Pierce, Palmer, Parkin, Bailey, Munro, McAlle, Sunderland, Hibbitt, Richards, Dougan, Wagstaffe (Powell)

Summerbee and Lee come off the field.

Manchester City: Macrae, Pardoe, Donachie, Doyle, Booth, Towers, Summerbee, Bell, Lee, Law, Marsh
Sub: Carradus

Referee: E.D. Wallace (Crewe)

Season: 1973/74

P	W	D	L	F	A	PTS
42	14	12	16	39	46	40

Division:	One
Position:	Fourteenth
Manager:	Johnny Hart/Ron Saunders
Top Goalscorer:	Francis Lee (18)
Average Attendance:	30,652

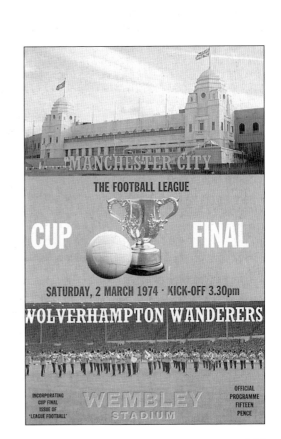

Match programme for the 1974 Cup Final.

MANCHESTER CITY V. NEWCASTLE UNITED

28 February 1976

Football League Cup Final
Wembley, London
Attendance: 100,000

Manchester City 2   Newcastle United 1
Barnes, Tueart   *Gowling*

Wembley day could have not come soon enough for the City fans, who had experienced a drought of six years without a trophy. City's opponents, Newcastle United, were a lowly First Division team.

The team's confidence was high as they went into the final. They had been tucked away on a health farm in the Chilterns, their only slight concern being Dave Watson's troublesome back. The week before the Cup Final, however, proved to be a dramatic one for Newcastle. They had really been affected by a flu bug and probably had the worst build-up any side has had to a final, losing no less than six players.

It was an open game right from the kick-off. Newcastle laid early siege to the Blues goal, with Joe Corrigan having to make two fine saves in the opening couple of minutes, and then having to turn a Malcolm MacDonald shot behind for a corner. The Blues were struggling to find any kind of rhythm.

On twelve minutes, City were awarded a free-kick for a foul on former first-team manager, Joe Royle. Mike Doyle headed Asa Hartford's free-kick back across the box and the ball fell invitingly for Peter Barnes, who smashed it home with his left foot.

Tommy Booth and Alan Oakes both then had shots wide of the target. Newcastle levelled the scores with ten minutes to go before half time. Hartford lost possession to Alan Kennedy on City's right wing and the ball was worked across the pitch to MacDonald, whose cross was turned in past Corrigan by the outstretched leg of Alan Gowling.

Dennis Tueart had a couple of opportunities to restore City's lead, but it was to no avail, and the teams went on level terms at the break. By all accounts, this was a fair indication of the opening forty-five minutes.

Two minutes after the interval, Tueart scored one of the most spectacular goals ever seen at Wembley. Booth headed a Willie Donachie cross towards Tueart, who had his back to goal, and a superb overhead kick flew past a diving Mahoney into the corner of the net.

Royle then chipped the ball over the 'keeper, but the goal was disallowed for offside.

There was no shortage of incidents in the final few minutes, as both sides had opportunities to score. In the final minute, Booth had a chance to seal the game, only to see his header saved.

Doyle led the victorious side up the famous Wembley steps to receive the Football League Cup from the Duke of Norfolk. The victory was the end result of a solid team performance

From left to right, back row: Royle, Oakes, Corrigan, Bell, Booth. Middle row: Book, Bailey, Donachie, Clements, Viljeon, Watson, -?- (trainer). Front row: Keegan, Hartford, Doyle, Tueart, Barnes.

and revenge for the FA Cup Final defeat at Newcastle's hands in 1955. It was a delight to see that eight of the twelve players had progressed from the club's youth policy.

Manchester City: Corrigan, Keegan, Donachie, Doyle, Watson, Oakes, Barnes, Booth, Royle, Hartford, Tueart

Newcastle United: Mahoney, Nattrass, Kennedy, Barrowclough, Keeley, Howard, Burns, Cassidy, McDonald, Gowling, Craig

Referee: J.K. Taylor (Wolverhampton)

Tony Book recalled, 'By now I was manager, and what sticks out most were the goals. The first was one we had worked on in training, when Mick Doyle pulled round the back from a free-kick and headed it across the goal for Peter Barnes to do the business, as for Dennis Tueart's overhead kick, it was just phenomenal.'

Season: 1975/76

P	W	D	L	F	A	PTS
42	16	12	15	64	46	43

Division:	One
Position:	Eighth
Manager:	Tony Book
Top Goalscorer:	Dennis Tueart (24)
Average Attendance:	34,281

Manchester City v. Chelsea

26 November 1977

Football League First Division
Maine Road, Manchester
Attendance: 34,345

Manchester City 6	Chelsea 2
Tueart (3)	*R. Wilkins*
Barnes, Channon	*Britton (pen)*
G. Wilkins (og)	

Under the management of Tony Book, City made every effort to win the Championship after finishing second the previous season. What was even more remarkable was that Denis Tueart, now a director at City, played only 17 games but scored 12 goals. He finished joint-second top scorer, but achieved a large percentage of his goals through scoring three hat-tricks.

The first hat-trick was away at Aston Villa in a 4-1 win in the second League game of the season. Then, in December, in a home fixture against Newcastle United, he scored another one. The third and final hat-trick arrived in an incredible game against Chelsea.

Due to the reputation of Chelsea's notorious travelling supporters, City made the decision to make the game all-ticket, so many fans missed a goal-scoring bonanza.

City took the lead on ten minutes with an incredible own goal. There seemed absolutely no danger when Peter Bonetti rolled the ball out to Graham Wilkins, but with Peter Barnes

Left: *Dave Watson signed for City from Sunderland and played in 190 games between 1975-79, scoring 6 goals.* Right: *Dennis Tueart spent two periods with City: 1974-78 and 1980-83. He played in a total of 267 games and scored 112 goals.*

rushing in on Wilkins, he chose to push the ball back to the 'keeper, only to find he was stranded yards out from his goal line. The ball trickled agonizingly over the line, despite the Chelsea 'keeper making a desperate attempt to clear it as he scrambled back.

Four minutes later, the Blues got a second goal. Bonetti let a Brian Kidd shot slip from his grasp, Barnes hooked it back in and Tueart made no mistake from close in. However, the goal only stood after the referee consulted his linesman.

Chelsea then hit back in the twenty-fourth minute, when Ray Wilkins scored with a shot which went in off a post to put his team right back in the game. Paul Power then hit a post for City, before Chelsea equalised on twenty-eight minutes. The referee had no hesitation in awarding a penalty when Kenny Clements tripped Swain in the box. Britton duly hit home the spot kick.

Right on the half-hour mark, the Blues of Manchester went into the lead again from a thundering Tueart shot and, a minute before half time, City regained their two-goal advantage. Barnes cut in from the right and rolled an inch-perfect pass to the feet of Mike Channon, whose shot was deflected past Bonetti by a Chelsea defender.

Within seconds of the restart, City almost had a fifth, but Channon saw his shot cannon off the inside of the post back into play. It was not long, though, before a fifth goal did arrive. Barnes, who was having an inspiring game, hit a low shot crisply, which practically sizzled into the bottom right-hand corner.

Hartford then struck the underside of the bar, as City continually looked like scoring with every attack. The Chelsea players were totally demoralized and this was highlighted by a touchline mêlée. Aylott crashed into Kidd, and this sparked a fracas when players from both sides joined in with fists and legs flying around.

The final goal of the game came courtesy of Tueart, who claimed his hat-trick, which concluded an incredible match full of fascinating football.

Manchester City: Corrigan, Clements, Donachie, Booth, Watson, Power, Barnes, Channon, Kidd, Hartford, Tueart
Sub: Keegan

Chelsea: Bonetti, G Wilkins, Sparrow, Britton, Droy, Wicks, Aylott, R Wilkins, Langley, Swain, Cooke,
Sub: Lewington

Referee: K. McNally (Mold)

Manager Tony Book, before the start of the game, said: 'It's vital we start winning games, today is a good time to start. We are only two points worse off than at this time last season, so the position is not completely irretrievable.'

Season: 1977/78

P	W	D	L	F	A	PTS
42	20	12	10	74	51	52

Division:	One
Position:	Fourth
Manager:	Tony Book
Top Goalscorer:	Brian Kidd (20)
Average Attendance:	41,687

AC Milan v. Manchester City

23 November 1978

UEFA Cup, Third Round, First Leg
San Siro Stadium, Milan, Italy
Attendance: 40,000

AC Milan 2   Manchester City 2
Bigon (2)   *Kidd, Power*

The first leg took place in the impressive San Siro stadium, but did not actually start as planned. The game should have been played on Wednesday 22 November, but the weather conditions were poor, with thick swirling fog forcing the referee to postpone the match before it started, disappointing the large number of supporters who had already gathered in the stadium. On the Thursday night, there were fewer fans in the ground than the previous night.

Milan had a perfect opportunity to score in the first minute, but full-back Collovat shot wide. Brian Kidd might have scored for City after only six minutes. City started to gain the upper hand and the Blues seemed more likely to score. On thirty-eight minutes, Asa Hartford sent the ball across to the unmarked Brian Kidd, who simply headed past 'keeper Enrico Albertosi. It was a fully deserved lead at the interval, and all other decent goal attempts had come to no avail, in particular when Albertosi made a spectacular save from Hartford three minutes before half time.

City refused to be intimidated either by the crowd or a curiously casual Milan attack. In the twelfth minute of the second half, City increased their lead with an incredible goal from Paul Power. He set off on a lengthy run with the ball, looking up occasionally to find a target. The Milan defenders kept retreating, so Power continued his run into the penalty area and fired in a low left shot which bounced over the diving body of the 'keeper. It gave City an unbelievable lead. Only two teams had ever defeated Milan in 52 European meetings at the San Siro, and no British side had ever beaten them. City seemed poised to make history.

Milan halved the lead within two minutes of City scoring, when Albertino Bigon forced the ball over the line from Walter Novellino's cross. City then came close to scoring again, when a Colin Bell shot skimmed the bar. The Italian side then stepped up the tempo in trying to preserve their European home record. Corrigan was beaten three times, but each time the linesman's flag was raised for offside. The decisions disgusted the volatile crowd, who pelted Corrigan with beer cans and bottles. With only eight minutes of the game left, Bigon scored his second goal for Milan to bring the scores level. Corrigan then had to make fine saves from Bigon and Chiodi, as City survived the nerve-wracking last few minutes.

This was the best ever performance given by City in Europe, but one which sparked off a riot outside the San Siro stadium which was only quelled when police and troops used tear gas and rubber bullets.

City were thus deprived of the distinction of becoming the first British team to win in the fearsome and almost frightening San Siro stadium. In a masterly and thoroughly professional performance, an under-strength City team played with an authority that stunned AC Milan.

AC Milan: Albertosi, Collovati, Maldera, De Vecchi, Bet, Baresi, Buriani, Bigon, Novellino, Rivera, Chiodi
Subs: Rigamonti (GK), Minoia, Boldina, Antonelli, Sartori

An article taken from an Italian newspaper showing how the teams lined up.

Cosi in campo ore 20,30	
MILAN	**MANCHESTER CITY**
ALBERTOSI **1**	CORRIGAN
COLLOVATI **2**	CLEMENTS
MALDERA **3**	DONACHIE
DE VECCHI **4**	BOOTH
BET **5**	WATSON
BARESI **6**	FUTCHER PAUL
BURIANI **7**	VILJOEN
BIGON **8**	PALMER
NOVELLINO **9**	KIDD
RIVERA **10**	HARTFORD
CHIODI **11**	BARNES

PANCHINA: 12. Rigamonti, 13. Boldini, 14. Minola, 15. Antonelli, 16. Sartori (All.: Liedholm). | PANCHINA: 12. McGreg, 13. Henroy, 14. Bell, 15. ·····. 16. Keegan (All.: Book).

Arbitro: Einbeck (Germania Est)
Guardalinee Kirschen e Scheukell

RADIO - Cronaca diretta alle 20,25 sulla Rete 1.

City's goalscorers in Italy were Power and Kidd. In this photograph, three Milan defenders watch helplessly as Power scores his side's opening goal.

Manchester City: Corrigan, Clements, Donachie, Booth, Watson, Owen, Keegan, Bell, Kidd, Hartford, Palmer
Subs: Macrae (GK), Futcher, Viljeon, Henry, Coughlin

Referee: H. Einbeck (East Germany)

Paul Power recalled, 'The game against AC Milan should have been played on the Wednesday evening, we got to the San Siro and got stripped, but a fog descended like you would not believe. They kept us there for an hour, hoping to start the game, but it was impossible, so the match was rescheduled for the Thursday afternoon. Many of the local supporters were at work, so with the stadium not full the atmosphere was not as intense as it would have been the previous evening, which suited us. We went two goals up, and though Milan pulled the match level, it was a great result and a tremendous performance. In the return, we were always on top and beat them comfortably 3-0.'

Season: 1978/79

P	W	D	L	F	A	PTS
42	13	13	16	58	56	39

Division: One
Position: Fifteenth
Manager: Tony Book
Top Goalscorer: Mick Channon (15)
Average Attendance: 36,202

HALIFAX TOWN v. MANCHESTER CITY

5 January 1980

FA Cup, Third Round
The Shay, Halifax
Attendance: 12,559

Halifax Town 1   Manchester City 0
Hendrie

The horror of Halifax was a disaster unparalleled in the history of City. It was a return to those bad old days of Maine Road, and to the dark days suffered in the Second Division of the early 1960s.

Malcolm Allison had assembled a team of expensive stars and Halifax were no more than an average Fourth Division side.

Farcical conditions ruined the match as a spectacle. Ground staff had been working on the pitch to clear surface water right until the kick-off, but the mud was still literally ankle deep. The outcome was that any superior skill City possessed was completely reduced to nothing.

The game got under way and, in the twenty-fifth minute, City created the best move of the opening exchanges so far. Paul Power sent a cross into Bobby Shinton, and a fine effort saw the Halifax goalkeeper gliding through the air to hold the ball magnificently. A minute later, Mike Robinson drove in a powerful shot only to see Kilner make a superb reflex-action save.

City looked to be in control of the game and the side's superior skill was becoming increasingly evident. Both sides were striving to break the deadlock as the abysmal conditions slowly took their toll. City tried to take advantage of their superior fitness by increasing the pressure after the break and were denied for a third occasion on sixty-four minutes by Kilner, as he stooped low to his left to hold a close effort from Shinton.

Then, in the seventy-fifth minute, the unthinkable happened when Halifax counter-punched devastatingly to take the lead. Andy Stafford, a former City schoolboy, crossed from the left and Smith knocked the ball back to Paul Hendrie, who drove the ball past Joe Corrigan. It was a severe blow. The goal seemed to give Halifax a new lease of life and every time City hit back, the home side would have nine men in defence.

Frustrations began to boil over, not just on the pitch but also in the stands. Several arrests were made as City fans were ejected from the ground, unable to find any excuses for what was becoming a barren,

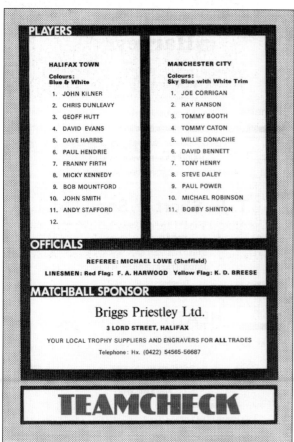

Look at the contrast in team line-ups.

Tommy Booth signed for City from Middleton Boys and played in 487 games between 1965-1981, scoring 36 goals.

frustrating and bitterly disappointing season, not to mention the abject failure to beat a poor home side. On the pitch, City were clearly frustrated at their attempts to retain control of a tie that was well within their capabilities, and in the dying seconds Tommy Caton had a shot blocked and Steve Daley followed up, blazing his effort wide. That just about summed up the day.

It was a black Saturday. FA Cup defeat by a mid-table Fourth Division side was a shattering blow to morale, as the club went on a run of 18 games without a win. It was one of the most humiliating defeats in the history of the club.

Halifax Town:
Kilner, Dunleavy, Hutt, Evans, Harris, Hendrie, Firth, Kennedy, Mountford, Smith, Stafford
Sub: Goodman

Manchester City:
Corrigan, Ranson, Power,Henry, Caton, Reid, Viljoen, Shinton, Robinson, Daley, D Bennett
Sub: Lee

Referee: M. Lowe (Sheffield)

Paul Power: 'Halifax was one of those games where it should not have been played at all. The pitch was an absolute bog. I remember we played a ball across the Halifax area, the goalkeeper had been completely beaten by the cross and Bobby Shinton needed only to tap it in, but the ball stopped in the mud. That would have given us the lead, but they nicked a goal. That and the Shrewsbury defeat, also in the FA Cup, were by far the biggest disappointments during my time at the club.'

Season: 1979/80

P	W	D	L	F	A	PTS
42	12	13	17	43	66	37

Division:	One
Position:	Seventeenth
Manager:	Malcolm Allison
Top Goalscorer:	Michael Robinson (9)
Average Attendance:	35,245

117

MANCHESTER CITY V. LIVERPOOL

14 January 1981

League Cup, Semi-Final, First Leg
Maine Road, Manchester
Attendance: 48,045

Manchester City 0   Liverpool 1
                               Kennedy

Manchester City were hoping to avoid a heavy defeat against an all-powerful Liverpool in the first leg of the League Cup semi-final. City's League Cup record (three finals, two wins and one defeat) was sternly put to the test by a Liverpool side aiming to capture the one trophy to have eluded Anfield.

City ran themselves magnificently into the ground in the first half, when they reduced Liverpool to a disorganized gang who never knew quite what had hit them. They were desperately unlucky to have what seemed a perfectly legal fourth-minute goal ruled out by the referee, the first of many decisions that were to bemuse the Maine Road faithful. The official adjudged that Kevin Reeves had fouled Kennedy in jumping for the ball, although it was hard to see how, and there was not one single complaint from any Liverpool player as Reeves ran away in delight to celebrate his goal.

Liverpool 'keeper Ray Clemence then had to be alert on eighteen minutes when he came charging off his goal line to smother the ball at the feet of Phil Boyer. A hint of a Liverpool threat came on thirty minutes when Kenny Dalglish drove the ball through for David Fairclough to test Joe Corrigan.

One further chance fell City's way when Paul Power rifled in a fierce left-foot drive that skimmed the post. Liverpool were implementing masterful tactics, allowing City to force the game but, at the same time, limiting them to creating hardly any worthwhile openings. After the match, City manager John Bond commented: 'We did not have enough experience and know-how to keep things going for ninety minutes.'

Liverpool then began calmly to pick City off, and Corrigan was forced to save a Graeme Souness blockbuster at the second attempt. On eighty-one minutes, the referee caused further controversy when he harshly penalized City skipper Power for a foul on Sammy Lee, that provided Liverpool with a free-kick from which Ray Kennedy serenely side-footed home Terry McDermott's cross. Three minutes from time, Lee should have scored a second for Liverpool.

While John Bond would have liked to have taken a handsome lead to Anfield for the second leg, he was confident that City could score an early goal in the return game and make things even, believing then his side would go on and win at fortress Anfield in a one-off situation.

History was not to be, but City earned a creditable 1-1 draw, with Kevin Reeves scoring for City and both fans and players were left to rue the controversial decisions of the referee from the first leg.

Manchester City: Corrigan, Ranson, Reid, Caton, Henry, Bennett, Power, Tueart, Mackenzie, Reeves, Boyer
Sub: Buckley

Liverpool: Clemence, Neal, A Kennedy, Thomson, R Kennedy, Irwin, Dalglish, Lee, Fairclough, McDermott, Souness
Sub: Case

Referee: A.W. Grey (Great Yarmouth)

MANCHESTER CITY

LIVERPOOL
MATCH MAGAZINE

TONIGHT'S MATCH IS SPONSORED BY

WEDNESDAY, 14th JANUARY 1981
KICK-OFF 7-45 p.m.
At Maine Road, Manchester
Football League Cup—Semi-Final 1st leg

30p

Assistant Chief John Benson: 'A quickie for us in the second leg at Anfield next month would be interesting … it would be even-stevens then. It's half time, we've got to kick up hill and against the wind'.

Season: 1980/81

P	W	D	L	F	A	PTS
42	14	11	17	56	59	39

Division:	One
Position:	Twelfth
Manager:	Malcolm Allison/John Bond
Top Goalscorer:	Kevin Reeves (17)
Average Attendance:	33,492

119

Manchester City v. Ipswich Town

11 April 1981

FA Cup Semi-Final
Villa Park, Birmingham
Attendance: 46,537

Manchester City 1   Ipswich Town 0
Power

City had really not wanted to draw Ipswich Town in the semi-final because Town were on such a good run and, at the time, were going for the treble. They had led the First Division for much of the season, as well as being in the semi-final of the FA Cup. They were also through to the last four of the UEFA Cup. Indeed, Ipswich were a force to be reckoned with, especially under the management of Bobby Robson.

There was a packed house at Villa Park on the day of the game. It was a hot day and the pitch was very firm. The majority of City's vast travelling army of fans were packed into one side of the Holte End. The atmosphere was electric.

On paper, Ipswich were the more fancied side and, as was expected, began the game the stronger and more stylish side of the two. Eric Gates and Alan Brazil both missed good chances, and Kevin Beattie should have opened the scoring before leaving the field of play with a broken arm on twenty-five minutes. He rose, unchallenged, to a set-piece, but his downward header was so powerful that it bounced over the bar.

Gradually, the Blues got into the game and a Paul Power shot rebounded off Paul Cooper and was cleared by John Wark, who had once had trials at City.

There were not many more clear chances for either side for the rest of the match and, on ninety minutes, the whistle blew.

At this point in time, the game witnessed an amusing incident. As soon as the referee

Paul Power scores the winning goal.

had blown his whistle, Ipswich's influential player Gates took his boots off, put them under his arm and begun to walk off the field of play, unaware that extra time had to be played.

Eleven minutes into extra time, and City won a free kick just outside the Ipswich penalty area, after England international Terry Butcher unceremoniously clattered into Dave Bennett.

Steve Mackenzie rolled the ball to Paul Power – a tactic City had worked on in training. Power hit a curving shot with his left foot and the ball flew over the fingertips of the despairing Cooper into the far corner. The Holte End erupted, and Blues in other stands were delirious.

If extra time was a bonus for City, it was a sentence of hard labour on Ipswich, who were clearly drained to the point of exhaustion.

The knowledge that City were actually going to Wembley was amazing. They were going to have the honour of taking part in the Centenary Final of the game's most famous knock-out competition.

Paul Power said of his goal, after the game: 'I have to admit it is the most memorable and satisfying goal I have scored.' I am sure not many City supporters would argue with that.

Manchester City: Corrigan, Ranson, McDonald, Reid, Power, Caton, Bennett, Gow, Mackenzie, Hutchison, Reeves
Sub: Booth

Ipswich Town: Cooper, Mills, Butcher, Thijssen, Osman, Beattie, (McCall), Wark, Muhren, Mariner, Brazil, Gates

Referee: P. Partridge (Cockfield, County Durham)

Paul Power: 'We were real underdogs for the match because Ipswich, under Bobby Robson, were a real force that season and were going for the treble of League, FA Cup and UEFA Cup. However, we played hard as a team, and, for me, Gerry Gow played particularly well that day. We got a free-kick in extra time, and I had a pop at goal that flew in. They had no time to get back in the game and we were at Wembley. From my point of view it was, without doubt, the most important goal I scored for City.'

Manchester City v. Tottenham Hotspur

9 & 14 May 1981

FA Cup Final
Wembley Stadium, London
Attendance: 99,500

Manchester City 1	Tottenham Hotspur 1
Hutchison	*Hutchison (og)*

FA Cup Final replay
Attendance: 92,500

Manchester City 2	Tottenham Hotspur 3
Mackenzie	*Villa (2)*
Reeves (pen)	*Crooks*

Much had been made about it being the Chinese year of the Cockerel and how Spurs always won major competitions in the years ending with one. It was also the Centenary FA Cup final, but all the Blues were left with was the memory of what might have been, after two gripping encounters in which they had success snatched from their grasp each time – a 1-1 extra-time draw, followed by an exciting replay which saw City go down by the odd goal in five.

In the first game, City opened the scoring on twenty-nine minutes. An exciting exchange of passes between Dave Bennett and Kevin Reeves found Ray Ranson, who sent in a teasing cross and Tommy Hutchison hurled himself forward to head home from some distance. City continued to control the majority of play, with Joe Corrigan proving his worth on the odd occasion. In the fifty-eighth minute, Steve Mackenzie almost made it two when an effort struck the post. Ten minutes from time, disaster struck when a Glenn Hoddle free kick struck Hutchison on the shoulder, and the ball deflected across the goal for a Spurs equalizer. It was a tragic own goal that threw Tottenham a lifeline. Two weary teams played an uneventful period of extra-time, and a replay the following Thursday was necessary.

In the replay, Tottenham again came from behind, this time to win. However, they opened the scoring on seven minutes when Ricky Villa had the simple chance of putting a ball away that Corrigan allowed to squirm out of his reach, following a Steve Archibald shot. Three minutes later, City equalized with the type of goal that would normally win finals when Steve Mackenzie scored with a tremendous 20-yard volley. City then took a sensational lead, when Kevin Reeves slotted home a penalty after Dave Bennett had been bundled over by Miller in the box. City desperately needed a third goal to give them a cushion against a Tottenham comeback.

WEMBLEY BOUND

MANCHESTER CITY'S PATH TO THE 100TH F.A. CUP FINAL

THIRD ROUND
Saturday, January 3rd
Manchester City 4   Crystal Palace 0   39,347
Reeves 2 (1 pen), Boyer, Power
Team: Corrigan; Ranson, Caton, Reid, Power, Reeves, Mackenzie, McDonald, Hutchison, Gow, Boyer.

FOURTH ROUND
Saturday, January 24th
Manchester City 6   Norwich City 0   36,919
Reeves, Gow, Mackenzie, Bennett, Power, McDonald.
Team: Corrigan; Henry, McDonald, Booth, Power, Caton, Boyer (Bennett), Gow, Mackenzie, Hutchison, Reeves.

FIFTH ROUND
Saturday, February 14th
Peterborough United 0   Manchester City 1   27,780
Booth
Team: Corrigan; Henry, Booth, Reid, McDonald, Hutchison, Gow, Mackenzie, Power, Reeves, Bennett.

SIXTH ROUND
Saturday, March 7th
Everton 2   Manchester City 2   52,791
Eastoe, Ross (pen)   Gow, Power
Team: Corrigan; Ranson, McDonald, Reid, Power, Caton, Tueart, Gow, Mackenzie, Hutchison, Reeves.

REPLAY
Wednesday, March 11th
Manchester City 3   Everton 1   52,532
McDonald 2, Power   Eastoe
Team: Corrigan; Ranson, McDonald, Reid, Power, Caton, Tueart, Gow, Mackenzie, Hutchison, Reeves.

SEMI-FINAL
Saturday, April 11th (at Villa Park, Birmingham)
Manchester City 1   Ipswich Town 0   46,537
Power
Team: Corrigan; Ranson, McDonald, Reid, Power, Caton, Bennett, Gow, Mackenzie, Hutchison, Reeves, Booth.

FINAL
Saturday, May 9th
Manchester City 1   Tottenham Hotspur 1   100,000
Hutchison   Hutchison (O.G.)
Team: Corrigan; Ranson, Caton, Reid, McDonald, Hutchison (Henry), MacKenzie, Gow, Power, Reeves, Bennett

The road to Wembley: the route to the Cup Final.

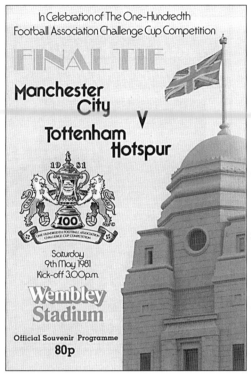

Both programmes are from the Centenary Cup final.

Garth Crooks levelled the scores on seventy minutes, and five minutes later came a goal of the sort that is only scored once in a lifetime. Villa wrong-footed several defenders and shot past Corrigan with one of the finest goals Wembley had ever seen. Manchester City may have lost at Wembley, but they won a host of new friends in one of the most memorable FA Cup finals of modern times.

Game 1

Manchester City: Corrigan, Ranson, McDonald, Reid, Power, Caton, Bennett, Gow, Mackenzie, Hutchison (Henry), Reeves

Tottenham Hotspur: Aleksic, Hughton, Miller, Roberts, Perryman, Villa (Brooke), Ardiles, Archibald, Galvin, Hoddle, Crooks

Game 2

Manchester City: Corrigan, Ranson, McDonald (Tueart), Caton, Reid, Gow, Power, Mackenzie, Reeves, Bennett, Hutchison

Tottenham Hotspur:
Aleksic, Hughton, Miller, Roberts, Perryman, Villa, Ardiles, Archibald, Galvin, Hoddle, Crooks

Referee: K. Hackett (Sheffield)

Paul Power: 'The final was so disappointing because we were nine minutes away from winning the cup, before Tommy Hutchinson's shoulder deflected a free-kick for their equalizer. In the replay, we recovered from a goal down to lead 2-1, but lost to Ricky Villa's goal, which everyone remembers. Personally, I'm sick of seeing it! That season, it was 100th FA Cup final and a great occasion to part of. I've never been jealous of anyone, but I was when Steve Perryman lifted the trophy that night. Looking back now, though, my memories are good ones'.

City players salute their fans.

Left: *Steve Mackenzie scored a spectacular goal in the replay.* Right: *Joe Corrigan signed as a schoolboy for City and played in 604 games.*

Stoke City v. Manchester City

5 September 1981

Football League First Division
Victoria Ground, Stoke
Attendance: 25,256

Stoke City 1   Manchester City 3
Chapman   *Francis (2)*
                         Boyer

The Blues had their best start to a campaign in years and were already looking to become Championship material. They had just completed the £1 million signing of Trevor Francis, and he quickly began the repayment of that massive fee.

Francis's first game for City was at Stoke. His appearance encouraged a massive following to go to the Victoria Ground, and the vast army almost doubled the normal Stoke attendance. The fans were packed in like sardines, and there were frequent requests over the tannoy system for people to move forward on the terracing to allow others in.

The injection of Francis clearly inspired City, and he received a fantastic ovation from the City following, as the players prepared to start the game.

Peter Fox in the Stoke goal was called upon early to save well from Francis, as well as Kevin Reeves and Martin O'Neill. Stoke had their moments too, in what was turning into a highly entertaining match, full of good football and endeavour. It was an all-action thriller, although later in the game the pace began to tell in such stamina-draining heat.

On the half-hour, a sizzling shot from Reeves brought another fine save from Fox, who was becoming the busier goalkeeper. Then, on thirty-five minutes, came the moment everyone had waited for: Bobby McDonald floated in a cross; and some neat skill by Francis had the crowd, who were basking in the sunshine, on their toes. He drew the advancing Fox off his line and slipped the ball between his legs to give City a deserved lead.

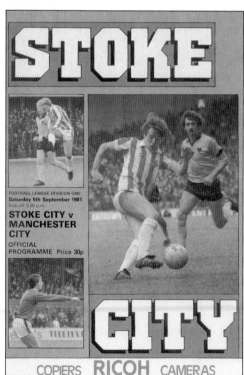

City made a flying start on resumption of the second half and within a minute, Reeves almost made it two, but Fox rushed off his line and spread his body to smother the shot. Stoke then equalised in the sixty-second minute. A long clearance from Fox was completely mistimed by Tommy Caton at the heart of the City defence, and Lee Chapman cleverly angled the ball past Joe Corrigan.

The response from City was instantaneous and Phil Boyer, a second-half substitute for Paul Power, restored the lead. With more clinical finishing, City could have had five or six goals, but Francis made an even more sensational impact, scoring in the final minute. He really was the difference between both teams. Altogether, it was a highly spectacular performance from a team who were trying to establish themselves at the top.

City eventually finished tenth in the final League table and Trevor Francis finished top scorer for the season.

Manchester City team c. 1981/2.

Stoke City: Fox, Evans, Hampton, Dodd, O'Callaghan, Doyle, Griffiths, Heath, Chapman, Bracewell, Maguire
Sub: Ursem

Manchester City: Corrigan, Ranson, McDonald, Reid, Power, Caton, O'Neill, Gow, Francis, Hutchison, Reeves
Sub: Boyer

Referee: L.M. Robinson (Sutton Coldfield)

Stoke boss Richie Barker, talking about Trevor Francis: 'He was the difference between the sides on Saturday.'

Season: 1981/82

P	W	D	L	F	A	PTS
42	15	13	14	49	50	58

Division:	One
Position:	Tenth
Manager:	John Bond
Top Goalscorer:	Trevor Francis (14)
Average Attendance:	34,063

Manchester City v. Luton Town

14 May 1983

Football League Division One
Maine Road, Manchester
Attendance: 42,843

Manchester City 0   Luton Town 1
                       Antic

Manchester City were relegated to the Second Division for the first time in twenty years following what can only be described as a disgraceful home defeat by Luton Town, which sparked after-match demonstrations from supporters who had stood by the club through thick and thin.

City only needed to draw to save themselves from being relegated, but Luton needed to win the game to avoid relegation.

The Blues received a tremendous welcome as they came out to a near-capacity crowd and stormed forward from the outset, but with so much at stake for both sides, the tension was razor sharp. Frustrations boiled over when Denis Tueart dived with enthusiasm at the edge of the penalty box, hoping for a spot kick. His actions angered the Luton players.

With a quarter of an hour gone, neither side had created a worthwhile chance. The Hatters were playing a containing game, the outcome of which was that chances remained thin on the ground, with both sides content to slug it out in midfield. Luton then slowly began to look the more composed side and began to look menacing in attack, with Paul Walsh, who later joined City, cannoning a shot into the side netting. City did make an attempt to pressurize their opponents in the minutes before the break, but Luton were able to clear comfortably.

City were indeed enjoying a charmed life, as they fought tenaciously for their First Division lives. It was becoming cliff-hanger stuff, with City adding to their own frustrations and anxious moments with sheer bad play and carelessness. Nerves of steel were needed but The Blues did not possess them, Luton remaining confidently composed and resilient. In the seventy-third minute Luton almost snatched the lead, when Stephens drove in a powerful angled shot that Alex Williams

could only parry. The ball hit Nicky Reid's foot and bounced on to the cross bar, and was so nearly a bizarre own goal. Three minutes from the end of this dramatic game, City were finally on their way down to the Second Division when substitute Antic shot Luton into the lead after yet another goalmouth scramble.

When the final whistle blew, Luton manager David Pleat danced a jig across the pitch, the City players raced off in disgrace and mounted police were called into break up running battles between supporters and Luton players.

City could never get the better of a Luton side who had clearly done their homework on the Blues, and the world of soccer was left to reflect on the sad and sorry decline of the once great and glamorous Manchester City Football Club. Paul Power recalled:

'I was partly at fault for the goal because I should have stopped the cross coming in. As for Antic's shot, I remember it was deflected past Alex Williams in goal.'

Manchester City: Williams, Ranson, McDonald, Reid, Bond, Caton, Tueart, Reeves, Baker (Kinsey), Hartford, Power

Luton Town: Godden, Stephens, Elliott, Horton, Goodyear, Donaghy, Hill, Aylott, Walsh, Turner, Stein (Antic)

Referee: A. Challinor (Rotherham)

Season: 1982/83

P	W	D	L	F	A	PTS
42	13	8	21	47	70	47

Division:	One
Position:	Twentieth
Manager:	John Bond/John Benson
Top Goalscorer:	David Cross (13)
Average Attendance:	26,788

David Pleat runs on to the pitch to celebrate his players' victory.

MANCHESTER CITY V. CHELSEA

23 March 1986

Full Members Cup Final
Wembley Stadium, London
Attendance: 68,000

Manchester City 4	Chelsea 5
Lillis (2, inc. pen)	*Speedie (3)*
Kinsey	*Lee (2)*
Rougvie (og)	

It had been five years since City had last appeared in a final at Wembley. This time they had fought their way through to the final stages of a competition which was seen by many as an unwanted encumbrance. It was commonly referred to as a 'Mickey Mouse' event, which was much maligned by the press who expected a half-empty Wembley for the final. They, however, underestimated the loyalty of City fans and their desire to see City succeed.

The final was not only well attended, but it also provided a high level of superlative entertainment, and Chelsea manager John Hollins was quoted as saying 'I've been to a few cup finals, but I've never seen a better one.'

An amazing 68,000 fans turned up to watch the match, as Chelsea took the honours with a 5-4 victory. Neither club had the most ideal preparations for the final, being forced to play matches twenty-four hours prior to the Wembley game. City drew 2-2 in a local derby against Manchester United, and Chelsea won 1-0 at Southampton. So, the sharp edge was missing from both teams.

City started brightly and, on nine minutes, Steve Kinsey put the Blues ahead and many supporters began to think that the trophy would be City's. David Speedie equalized from a Pat Nevin cross in the twenty-fourth minute to give Chelsea the initiative and, in the thirty-sixth minute, Colin Lee netted Chelsea's second goal to give them a merited half-time lead.

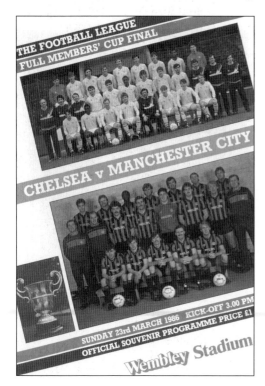

Minutes after the restart, Kinsey was tripped in the box by Chelsea defender McLaughlin, but the referee was not convinced it was a penalty and refused all appeals.

City were then swamped in the second half, with Speedie adding Chelsea's third goal on fifty-two minutes, and then completing his hat-trick on fifty-nine minutes. This was his first hat-trick since playing for Darlington in the Fourth Division, and he joined the elite club few who had scored hat-tricks in a Wembley final, including Stan Mortensen in the 1953 FA Cup final and Geoff Hurst in the 1966 World Cup final. After the match, Speedie claimed he should have had six and deserved his £1,000 win bonus.

City now looked dead and buried and when Lee drove in a 25-yarder in the eightieth minute, many City fans left, thinking Chelsea had an unassailable lead.

The introduction of England U-21 winger Paul Simpson changed things. A firm headed goal by Mark Lillis from a Simpson cross five minutes from time brought some respectability to the scoreline, but City were not finished. Doug Rougvie headed home another Simpson cross, although Lillis argued he had got the final touch. In the eighty-ninth minute, Lillis converted a penalty when Nigel Spackman tripped Andy May in the box.

Suddenly, there was the prospect of extra time and a penalty shoot-out. With City fighting to secure an equalizer, Chelsea were relieved to hear the final whistle. Another five minutes and City would surely have brought the scores level.

Manchester City: Nixon, Reid (Baker), Power, Redmond, McCarthy, Phillips (Simpson), Lillis, May, Kinsey, McNab, Wilson

Chelsea: Francis, Woods, Rougvie, Pates, McLaughlin, Bumstead, Nevin, Spackman, Lee, Speedie, McAllister

Referee: A. Saunders (Newcastle upon Tyne.)

Paul Power: 'We played Manchester United in a League game at Old Trafford, which we drew 2-2, the day before the final with Chelsea, so that had been a hard game for us. Chelsea had played Southampton, which had been easier really. Even so, we went 1-0 up, before finding ourselves 5-1 down. Mark Lillis then scored a twice for us to put us 5-4 down. Andy May then had a chance late on but missed so we nearly got a tremendous result, but it's always nice to play at Wembley.'

Season: 1985/86

P	W	D	L	F	A	PTS
42	11	12	19	43	57	45

Division:	One
Position:	Fifteenth
Manager:	Billy McNeil
Top Goalscorer:	Gordon Davies/ Mark Lillis (15)
Average Attendance:	24,219

City's route to their one and only appearance in the Full Members Cup final.

FULL MEMBERS' CUP TEAM LINE-UPS

14th October
Beat LEEDS UNITED Home 6-1
Attendance: 4,029
Nixon, Reid, Power, Clements, Johnson, May, Lillis, Baker, Davies (Melrose), McNab, Simpson (Tolmie).
Scorers: Davies 3, Power, Lillis, Baker.

22nd October
Beat SHEFFIELD UNITED Away 2-1
Attendance: 3,420
Nixon, May, Power, Reid, Johnson, Phillips, Lillis, Baker, Davie, McNab, McIlroy (Simpson).
Scorers: Phillips, Baker.

4th November
AREA SEMI-FINAL
Beat SUNDERLAND Home on penalties after 0-0 draw
Attendance: 6,642
Nixon, Reid, May, Clements, Johnson, Phillips, Lillis, Melrose (Smith), Davies (Moulden), Power, Simpson.

26th November
AREA FINAL First Leg
Lost to HULL CITY Away 1-2
Attendance: 5,213
Nixon, Reid, Power, Clements, McCarthy, Phillips, Melrose, May, Davies, McNab, Wilson (Simpson).
Scorer: Phillips.

11th December
AREA FINAL Second Leg
Beat HULL CITY Home 2-0
Attendance: 10,180
Nixon, Reid, Power, Clements, McCarthy, Phillips, Lillis, May, Davies, McIlroy, Simpson (Melrose).
Scorers: Phillips, Melrose.

Manchester City v. Huddersfield Town

7 November 1987

Football League Division Two
Maine Road, Manchester
Attendance: 19,583

Manchester City 10   Huddersfield Town 1
Stewart (3), Adcock (3),   *May (pen.)*
White (3), McNab

This was a game that will remain long in the memories of fans, and one of those matches that you may be telling your grandchildren about one day, not only for the nine-goal margin being the club's biggest ever in a League game, but also for the gruesome black-and-yellow-square kit sported by a Huddersfield Town team, who were languishing at the bottom of the League for their visit to Maine Road.

Despite their lowly League position, Huddersfield could have taken the lead twice in the opening ten minutes. However, once the influential Neil McNab had broken the deadlock, Huddersfield went to pieces and the floodgates opened.

Paul Simpson, a member of City's successful youth side, was concocting his magic on the left wing, and Paul Stewart doubled the scoring after twenty-nine minutes. Five minutes later, Tony Adcock headed the third, and just before the half-time interval, David White scored his first of the game and City's fourth.

The crowd was vibrant at half time and many ecstatic discussions were taking place between groups of friends – and complete strangers! The main topic of conversation was how many City would score in the second half.

The interval only prolonged the agony for the new Huddersfield manager, Malcolm McDonald, who was only into his third week in the job and must have been feeling utterly bemused and stunned by what he was witnessing.

In the fifty-second minute, Adcock scored his second. Then followed two goals in as many minutes: Stewart in the sixty-sixth minute and then Adcock's third goal of the game on sixty-seven.

It was a further seventeen minutes before the rampant Blues scored their eighth goal of the game, Stewart converting an Andy Hinchcliffe cross to complete his hat-trick. The last five minutes of the game produced three more goals and, perhaps, the biggest disappointment on the day: City failed to keep a clean sheet. Huddersfield pulled back a consolation goal in the eighty-eighth minute, with a penalty from Andy May, who had started his career at Maine Road. The ironic cheers that cascaded down from the Kippax stand suggested City fans were not complaining.

White scored his second on eighty-five minutes and there was still time for City's tenth, another from White as he dribbled the ball round a hapless Cox.

The lasting memories from this game must be literally every City fan buying the Sunday papers the following day and City having three hat-trick men, who were all rewarded with replica balls. The game did not promise to be the most glamorous of matches, but little did those City fans passing through the turnstiles know what lay ahead.

Manchester City: Nixon, Gidman, Hinchcliffe, Clements, Lake, Redmond, White, Stewart, Adcock, McNab, Simpson

Huddersfield Town: Cox, Brown, Bray, Banks, Webster, Walford, Barham, May, Shearer, Winter, Cork

Referee: K. Breen (Maghull)

City manager Mel Machin's commented after the match that 'it may take two or three years to grasp real success, but the future at City looks good. The groundwork has been done and we can now start to reach out in keen anticipation of bigger and better things.'

Season: 1987/88

P	W	D	L	F	A	PTS
44	19	8	17	80	60	65

Division:	Two
Position:	Ninth
Manager:	Mel Machin
Top Goalscorer:	Paul Stewart (28)
Average Attendance:	19,471

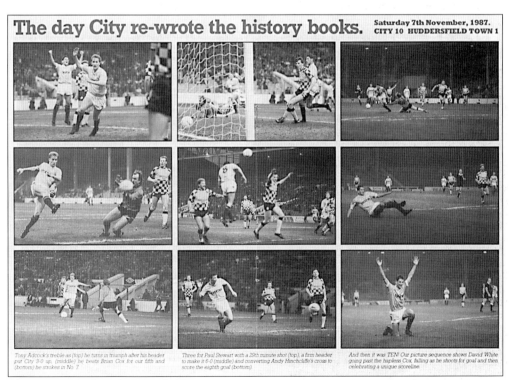

The day City re-wrote the history books. Saturday 7th November, 1987. CITY 10 HUDDERSFIELD TOWN 1

Tony Adcock's treble as (top) he turns in triumph after his header put City 3-0 up, (middle) he beats Brian Cox for our fifth and (bottom) he strokes in No.7.

Three for Paul Stewart with a 29th minute shot (top), a firm header to make it 6-0 (middle) and converting Andy Hinchcliffe's cross to score the eighth goal (bottom).

And then it was TEN! Our picture sequence shows David White going past the hapless Cox, falling as he shoots for goal and then celebrating a unique scoreline.

The ten City goals in this remarkable game.

Hull City v. Manchester City

27 August 1888

Football League Second Division
Boothferry Park, Hull
Attendance: 11,653

Hull City 1   Manchester City 0
Edwards

City started their second successive campaign in the Second Division, having finished ninth the previous season. Manager Mel Machin described the division as being 'the most fiercely competitive for years.' The division was full of teams all ready to contest promotion, and City were due to open their campaign at Hull. Making their Second Division debuts for the club were four new players: Andy Dibble, Brian Gayle, Wayne Biggins and Nigel Gleghorn.

The game was played at a time when supporters of all clubs were fighting against poor publicity and negative media focus. Something needed to be done to put the fun back into football, and this was the game when the inflatable craze finally arrived, with over half the crowd in possession of some form of inflatable.

In the opening spell of the game, City were the most impressive side and should have had a two-goal cushion. They missed a glorious chance to take the lead on fourteen minutes when a surging run from Paul Lake exposed the Hull defence and left City with the advantage of four against one. With only Hull goalkeeper Tony Norman to beat, Trevor Morley carelessly wasted the goalscoring opportunity when he saw his effort smothered by Norman.

City continued to be the more potent and positive side, failing only in front of goal. Gayle joined in the onslaught, heading narrowly wide. The greater class of City was always evident, as they continually forced Hull to soak up an enormous amount of pressure and, seconds before half time, Neil McNab's delicately chipped free-kick struck the post and came back into play.

Despite City's first-half superiority, they were made to pay for all their missed chances when, on

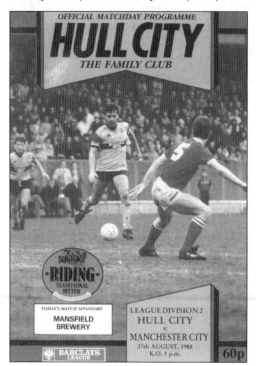

forty-seven minutes, Keith Edwards scored the 210th goal of his football career, swooping to connect with a lethal header past a stranded Dibble. City attempted to regain their composure and continued to pile on the pressure. Biggins hit the bar with a header and the anguish continued when further chances fell to David White and Morley, but both players failed to make them pay in front of goal.

City's luck was still against them even in the dying minutes, when Gayle saw a header bounce back off the crossbar.

Although City lost at Hull, it was generally accepted that the Blues had annihilated them and that the 1-0 defeat was a total injustice. Manchester City fans had also launched the craze for inflatables and, over the course of the next twelve months, most other clubs followed in some way or another, with some amusing and memorable away games at places like Stoke City on Boxing Day and the promotion party at Bradford City.

134

Hull City: Norman, Jobson, Jacobs, Warren, Skipper, Terry, Dyer, Roberts, Moore, Edwards, Saville
Subs: Palmer, De Mange

Manchester City: Dibble, Lake, Hinchcliffe, Gayle, Brightwell, Redmond, White, Biggins, Morley, McNab (Varadi), Gleghorn
Sub: Seagrave

Referee: S. Lodge (Barnsley)

Neil McNab, City's midfield general, told his team-mates 'Do not worry, we played brilliantly. We had more chances in that game than against Huddersfield when we won 10-1 at Maine Road the season before.'

The inflatable craze saw Fyffes taking out advertisements in City's match programme.

BRADFORD CITY v. MANCHESTER CITY

13 May 1989

Football League Second Division
Valley Parade, Bradford
Attendance: 12,479

Bradford City 1   Manchester City 1
Ellis   *Morley*

The Blues simply had to get a point from their last match to be certain of promotion. The remaining match was against a team placed fourteenth in the League, and surely with nothing to play for, Bradford City. It was a game that certainly caught the imagination of the City supporters and produced another fantastic away following, with City fans in every section of the ground.

Injuries to key defenders forced City to field a makeshift back four. It was little wonder, then, that City made a shaky start to the most crucial match of their season and it took the opening fifteen minutes of the game for the players involved to get an understanding.

Bradford pressed forward and The Blues simply panicked, conceding a goal on twenty-four minutes when Mark Ellis scored his first goal in nearly two years. City knew then that they were going to be in for a game.

The Blues stormed the Bradford defence and created chance after chance. David White raced into the heart of the Bradford defence and cracked a shot against the woodwork, and Trevor Morley had a handful of chances, which went everywhere but in the net.

During the half-time interval, various scorelines were filtering through from the delayed Crystal Palace *v.* Birmingham City game. Palace were the only team with a chance of overhauling City and they had already built up a four-goal lead. City fans feared the worst.

City totally dominated the second half, but became more and more frustrated at being

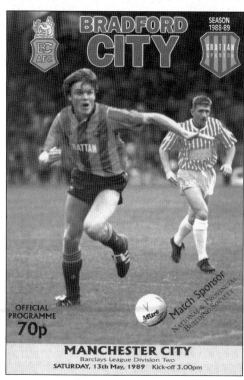

unable to find an equalizer. At times, it appeared more likely that Bradford would increase their lead as Paul Cooper had to make a brilliant save, dashing off his line to block a goal-bound shot.

For one City fan, the tension was too much and he ran on the pitch and pleaded with the players for more effort! With four minutes remaining, the Blues responded with a magical move. Cooper threw the ball out to Paul Moulden, he passed the ball out to White on the right, who sent in a cross, and Morley finally found the target after his string of earlier misses.

City had returned to the First Division, but they had left it late. The masters of suspense had kept their fans hanging on till the end, but City had finally made it after one of the cliff-hangers for which they had become famous. Bradford City manager Terry Yorath commented after the match: 'I am glad City made the point. The First Division needs clubs of their size and stature'.

Bradford City:
Tomlinson, Mitchell, Tinnion, Palin, Jackson, Evans, Campbell (Duxbury), Ellis, Leonard, Quinn, Abbott
Sub: Jewell

Manchester City:
Cooper, Lake, Hinchcliffe, Megson, Brightwell, Redmond, White, Moulden, Morley, McNab, Gleghorn
Subs: Oldfield, Taggart

Referee: P. Wright (Northwich)

Season: 1988/89

P	W	D	L	F	A	PTS
46	23	13	10	77	53	82

Division: Two
Position: Second
Manager: Mel Machin
Top Goalscorer: Paul Moulden (17)
Average Attendance: 23,500

A promotion special.

Manchester City v. Manchester United

23 September 1989

Barclays League First Division
Maine Road, Manchester
Attendance: 43,246

Manchester City 5   Manchester United 1
Oldfield (2)   *Hughes*
Morley, Bishop, Hinchcliffe

A list of City's greatest matches would not be complete without this match. To put things into perspective, a brief description of the background and the build-up to the match should remind City supporters of one of the most remarkable results in the history of derby football.

Mel Machin was the man who had guided City back into the First Division after an absence of two years. It looked as if it was going to be a difficult first season back. City had struggled in their opening six games and were languishing near the bottom of the League.

Things were somewhat different at Old Trafford. Their side contained several million-pound players and they were on the crest of a wave. Alex Ferguson, the United manager, had spent a lot of money purchasing players in the pursuit of a team to bring lasting success.

Throughout the build-up to the game, United fans, in particular the media and soccer pundits, predicted one result only: an easy victory to United. City's young side looked to have little chance against the big money buys, but the outcome was something very unexpected.

On a gloriously sunny afternoon, City never gave United an inch of room to work in. The players did not really need motivating, as it was evident from the start they wanted to win more than United did.

United opened brightly before some ugly crowd disturbances in the North Stand forced the players to leave the field of play. On returning to the pitch, City settled down the quicker of the two sides. David Oldfield and Trevor Morley were menacing in attack for the Blues.

Oldfield was left to score from 10 yards when Gary Pallister, a £2.3 million pre-season buy from Middlesborough, failed to clear an Andy Hinchcliffe cross. Then, a minute later, Morley pounced in the six-yard box after Jim Leighton had parried a Paul Lake shot. This left the Reds devastated and enabled City to gain a stranglehold on the game.

United attempted to rally, but City hit back on the counter in superb style, scoring a third goal on thirty-five minutes when Ian Bishop headed superbly past a bewildered Leighton, from an Oldfield cross.

The second half started in explosive style, Mark Hughes reducing the arrears with a magnificent bicycle-kick which flew over Paul Cooper into the net. City extended their lead with additional goals from Oldfield and a bullet header from Hinchcliffe.

It was a scintillating victory, made even sweeter as City leapfrogged United in the table on goal difference. The foundations of the victory were built on eleven players who contributed 100 per cent towards the pride and passion which won the game for City.

This is a result that City's long-suffering fans still talk about to this day: inflicting a humiliating defeat against their long-time rivals while recording their most convincing home victory in the history of derby League games.

It was sheer 'Blue murder,' as City eclipsed their expensive neighbours, who were made to look like sad and sorry millionaire misfits.

Manchester City
Cooper, Fleming, Hinchcliffe, Bishop, Gayle, Redmond, White, Morley, Oldfield, I. Brightwell, Lake (Beckford)
Sub: Megson

Manchester United
Leighton, Anderson, Donaghy, Duxbury, Phelan, Pallister, Beardsmore (Sharpe), Ince, McClair, Hughes, Wallace
Sub: Blackmore

Referee: N. Midgeley (Bolton)

City manager Mel Machin's after-match view was, 'if we can play like that once, we can play like that again. We have set ourselves a standard and it is one we must try to maintain. I was proud of my players. Proud of the way they approached the game and proud at the way they conducted themselves in achieving this splendid result.'

United manager Alex Ferguson's after-match view was 'it was the worst defensive performance in my time at United. We lost terrible goals. It was like trying to climb a glass mountain. The finishing of City was the deciding factor.'

Season: 1989/90

P	W	D	L	F	A	PTS
38	12	12	14	43	52	48

Division:	One
Position:	Fourteenth
Manager:	Mel Machin/Howard Kendall
Top Goalscorer:	Clive Allen/David White (14)
Average Attendance:	27,975

Manchester City v. Derby County

20 April 1991

Barclays League First Division
Maine Road, Manchester
Attendance: 24,037

Manchester City 2   Derby County 1
Quinn, White   *Harford*

Both teams were having contrasting fortunes: City were fourth in the top division and had only lost one of their previous seven games, whereas Derby County were desperately in need of a victory in their fight to avoid the drop to Second Division football.

Derby's 'keeper, the former England international, Peter Shilton pulled out just before the game with an injury and was replaced by Martin Taylor, a young and inexperienced 'keeper.

A bizarre and stormy match then unfolded before the eyes of the Maine Road faithful. Taylor was tested early on, when good play down the City left saw Neil Pointon cross on the run and Niall Quinn headed straight into the arms of the 'keeper.

In the twenty-second minute, City took the lead in a game Derby had to win to stand any chance of survival in the First Division when, from the edge of the penalty area, Quinn struck a low, left-foot volley into the corner of the net.

Then, just on the half-hour mark, Derby were thrown a lifeline. A long ball over the top of the City defence found Dean Saunders, who was adjudged to be onside. One on one with Tony Coton, the Welsh international took the ball to Coton's right and was brought down. The referee had no option but to promptly show Coton the red card for a professional foul. So incensed was Coton that he threw his gloves away in anger, one of them hitting the match official.

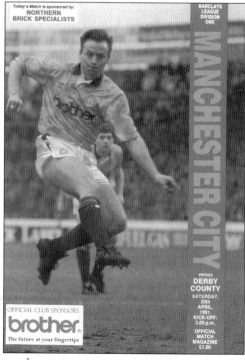

Left: *Niall Quinn, the hero of the day.* Right: *The match programme.*

The question on the astonished crowd's lips was who would go in goal. Up stepped Quinn, who was about to become an instant hero. Saunders himself took the penalty kick, low down and to the left, but Quinn guessed the right way and kept it out. All hope for Derby then faded away. A first half full of incident ended with just Quinn's earlier goal separating the sides.

In the second half, although down to ten men, City continued to make chances and Mark Wright had to be alert when he cleared a Pointon shot off the line. Manager Peter Reid then brought himself on to replace Mark Ward, who in his anger of being substituted kicked a bucket of water over and was left facing a club fine.

A minute later, David White effectively sealed the game as Derby handed City the second goal on a plate. Nick Pickering gave the ball away to David White, who ran past two defenders and crashed an unstoppable left-foot shot high into the net from just inside the 18-yard area, consigning Derby to Second Division football.

In the last minute of the game, Quinn was finally beaten when Mick Harford scored with a header, as Quinn was left stranded in no man's land. The goal was inadequate solace for a Derby team who had rarely put in a serious shot on Quinn.

Quinn had proved himself a hero in the one and only time he ever played in goal in a competitive game for City.

Manchester City: Coton, Hill, Pointon, Heath, Hendry, Redmond, White, Brennan, Quinn, Harper, Ward (Reid)
Sub: Allen

Derby County: Taylor, Sage, Pickering, Williams, Wright, Kavanagh (Cross), Micklewhite, Saunders, Harford, Wilson (Patterson), Williams

Referee: K. Lupton

Niall Quinn: 'As I was putting the jersey on, I then thought "what am I doing?" I got a bit nervous when I thought about the penalty. I remember Tony throwing his gloves away in anger, one of them hit the referee and then I picked them up and went in goal. I thought to myself "I'll have a laugh here. I probably won't save it, but I'll have a guess."'

Season: 1990/91

P	W	D	L	F	A	PTS
38	17	11	10	64	53	62

Division:	One
Position:	Fifth
Manager:	Howard Kendall/Peter Reid
Top Goalscorer:	Niall Quinn (22)
Average Attendance:	27,873

Manchester City v. Queens Park Rangers

17 August 1992

Premier League
Maine Road, Manchester
Attendance 24,471

Manchester City 1   Queens Park Rangers 1
White   *Sinton*

This game will be remembered more for the razzmatazz that was associated with it, rather than the action that took place on the field of play.

BSkyB were celebrating their £340 million live television deal, and this game was the first of their Monday night soccer service. Dancing girls, fireworks, the Red Devils (airborne variety) and blasting rock music helped give this match a real sense of occasion.

Rangers were determined to enjoy themselves in their own way, and refused to enter the party mood as they frustrated City. A mixture of good luck and stout defending enabled Rangers to hold out until six minutes from the interval, and then City broke the deadlock with the help of a slice of luck. Newcomer Rick Holden, a £900,000 signing from Oldham Athletic, crossed in from the left, Paul Lake – back after a two-year absence through injury – got an important touch to Niall Quinn, who fired in a low shot which Rangers 'keeper Jan Stejskal parried away. David White, City's 24-goal top scorer from the previous season, reacted the quickest. Using his pace, he rushed across the box and managed to squeeze the ball home at the far post, scoring a goal that City truly deserved.

The goal only hardened Rangers' resolve and, for much of the second half, they were the team that threatened, and they took the wind out of City's sails with a magnificent equalizer

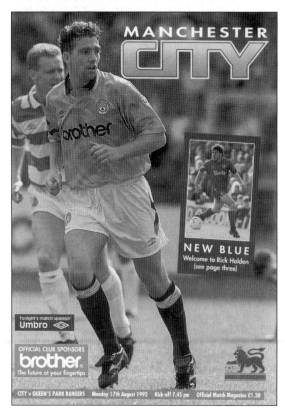

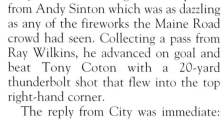

from Andy Sinton which was as dazzling as any of the fireworks the Maine Road crowd had seen. Collecting a pass from Ray Wilkins, he advanced on goal and beat Tony Coton with a 20-yard thunderbolt shot that flew into the top right-hand corner.

The reply from City was immediate: Fitzroy Simpson, City's Jamaican international, let fly with a cracker of his own which Stejskal tipped against the bar. QPR continued to force the game, but City had Coton to thank for a series of saves that prevented City from being defeated. Two saves were particularly important: one was a long-range effort from Wilkins and the other a close-range header from Darren Peacock.

The end of the game signalled another fireworks display and City looked back on the game. They had come perilously close to losing a match that, at one stage, they had threatened to win in style.

After the match, City manager Peter Reid commented: 'It was a fast and furious game, which must have entertained the fans. My players were disappointed because they went off the boil after the interval, after they had looked in control. The most satisfying aspect of the game from our point of view, was to see Paul Lake back in action. He got tired late on, which is understandable after being out for two years.'

Manchester City: Coton, Hill, Brightwell, Simpson, Curle, Vonk, White, Lake, Quinn, Holden, McMahon
Subs: Margetson (GK), Sheron, Flitcroft

Queens Park Rangers: Stejskal, Bardsley, Wilson, Wilkins, Peacock, McDonald, Impey, Holloway, Ferdinand, Bailey, Sinton

Referee: M. Bodenham (Cornwall)

Season: 1992/93

P	W	D	L	F	A	PTS
42	15	12	15	56	51	57

Division:	Premier
Position:	Ninth
Manager:	Peter Reid
Top Goalscorer:	David White (19)
Average Attendance:	24,698

Club captain Keith Curle.

MANCHESTER CITY V. TOTTENHAM HOTSPUR

22 October 1994

FA Carling Premiership
Maine Road, Manchester
Attendance: 25,473

Manchester City 5   Tottenham Hotspur 2
Walsh (2)   *Dumitrescu (2)*
Quinn, Lomas, Flitcroft

Many people who have looked back over classic matches in time have picked this game as one to remember, and quite rightly so.

This was a seven-goal thriller at Maine Road. Many City fans went into the game thinking that Tottenham's exciting and potent attacking options were more than a match-winning combination for any team, let alone City, with names like Jurgen Klinsmann, Teddy Sheringham, Ilie Dumitrescu, Jason Dozzell and Nick Barmby.

Tottenham made most of the running in the opening stages, but it was left to a former Spurs player, and now a lively target man for City, Paul Walsh, to open the scoring and stamp his personality on the game, when he pounced to sweep home a low shot from a well-placed Steve Lomas cross. Klinsmann hauled Spurs back into the match by earning a penalty after being pulled down by City 'keeper Andy Dibble, and Dumitrescu converted the spot kick.

City soon regained supremacy and, in the space of three minutes, scored two goals. Niall Quinn launched himself forward to head home a Walsh cross. Nick Summerbee then turned provider with a magnificent cross, and Walsh headed home with venom.

Spurs, to their credit, never relented and their resistance flickered briefly at the start of the second half, with Dumitrescu claiming his second goal.

City countered six minutes later, when Peter Beagrie unleashed an inch-perfect cross for

Steve Lomas to head home in style. Walsh had the last word: he ran at the heart of the Spurs defence, bamboozled three defenders and then rolled the ball back to Garry Flitcroft, who crashed home his shot.

Millions of BBC1's *Match of the Day* viewers, as well as a world-wide television audience, were certainly left with the name 'Manchester City' on their minds.

Manager Brian Horton commented after the match: 'The real winners were the paying public and the viewers around the world who watched the match on TV. You will not see a better game of soccer than that. There were great individual performances from players from both sides. All credit to Spurs, they did not try to shut up shop and stop us playing. They kept going forward looking for goals just like us.'

The crowd had been treated to a rare spectacle, and both teams left the pitch to a wholly deserved standing ovation.

 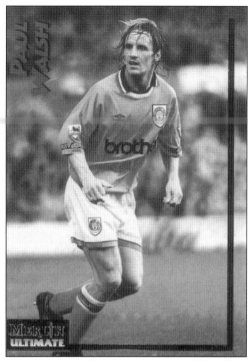

Left: *Garry Flitcroft progressed through City's youth ranks to play 134 games between 1989-1996, scoring 15 goals.* Right: *Former Spurs player Paul Walsh scored twice against his old club.*

Manchester City: Dibble, Edghill, I Brightwell, Curle, Phelan, Summerbee, Flitcroft, Lomas, Beagrie, Walsh, Quinn
Subs: Hill, Mike, Margetson

Tottenham Hotspur: Walker, Kerslake, Campbell, Scott, Edinburgh, Popescu, Dozzell, Dumitrescu, Barmby, Klinsmann, Sheringham

Referee: David Elleray

Season: 1994/95

P	W	D	L	F	A	PTS
42	12	13	17	53	64	49

Division:	Premier
Position:	Seventeenth
Manager:	Brian Horton
Top Goalscorer:	Uwe Rosler (22)
Average Attendance:	22,725

Manchester City v. Notts County

19 August 1998

Worthington Cup, Round One, Second Leg
Maine Road, Manchester
Attendance: 10,063

Manchester City 7	Notts County 1
Goater (2), Dickov (2)	*Torpey*
Mason, Bradbury, Whitley	

City's recent decline in fortunes over the years meant the club had to enter the old League Cup (now sponsored by Worthington's) at its qualifying stages for the first time in its history.

An unspectacular start to their first season in the Nationwide League Division Two put added pressure on the team to be successful in the cup competitions.

Supporters need not have worried, though, as City cruised through to the second round of the competition with an awesome display of finishing that enabled them to over run Notts County in a one-sided tie. The alarm bells that had been ringing the week before this tie were switched off, as they dismantled the previous season's Division Three champions and rewrote the record books with their best ever League Cup victory.

Youth team player Gary Mason scored City's first goal of the night, when he raced onto Shaun Goater's pass. Paul Dickov then capitalized on some poor defending and slid home Richard Edghill's cross. The Blues then wasted several opportunities to increase their lead, before Lee Bradbury took the first steps towards paying back his £1.5 million transfer fee, when he accepted a through-ball from Dickov and beat Ward in the Notts County goal. Goater scored a fourth goal for City with a spectacular volley.

The one-way traffic continued after the break. Dickov was a thorn in the Magpies side, and the live wire striker scored a fifth goal for City on fifty-eight minutes. The pressure was

unrelenting, and substitute Jim Whitley scored a sixth with a free shot on goal. Nicky Weaver was having a quiet time in the City goal and rarely saw any action, although his missed punch did allow Torpey to head home a consolation goal. Goater then made it seventh heaven for the fans in the dying seconds.

Joe Royle commented after the game: 'City's fans really deserve something like that, after all the problems they have had to witness. It's been a long time coming for them, and I hope they enjoyed it. This result was for the fans. They have not seen too many results like this in recent years, so it was something for them to savour.'

Manchester City:
Weaver, Edghill, Horlock (Jim Whitley), Fenton, Wiekens, Vaughan, Mason, Pollock,

Danny Allsopp joined City from Australian club Port Melbourne Sharks in 1998, before moving to Notts County in 2000.

Nick Fenton progressed through City's ranks before joining Notts County.

Goater, Dickov (Allsopp), Bradbury (Conlon)
Subs: Wright (GK), Jeff Whitley, Brown

Notts County: Ward, Fairclough, Owers, Redmile, Billy (Dudley), Hughes, Murray, Robson (Dyer), Liburd, Jones (Henshaw), Torpey
Subs: Beattie, Tierney

Referee: M. Jones (Chester)

MANCHESTER CITY V. MANSFIELD TOWN

8 December 1998

Auto Windscreens Shield, Northern Section, First Round
Maine Road, Manchester
Attendance: 3,007

Manchester City 1   Mansfield Town 2
Allsopp   *Peacock (2, inc. pen)*

City were onto a hiding to nothing against a team who, in their previous fixture, had just been knocked out of the FA Cup by non-League opposition. City made a host of changes to their side, the most notable being the inclusion of giant defender Stephen Rimmer for his first ever game. Rimmer was a product of the flourishing youth development system at City.

An out of the ordinary atmosphere hung over Maine Road as the match kicked off in a near deserted stadium. City began brightly and, with barely sixty seconds gone, Neil Heaney narrowly failed to connect to a Danny Allsopp through-ball. Allsopp should have put the Blues ahead on seven minutes, but he pushed a Jeff Whitley cross wide. The young Australian then had two further opportunities to open the scoring. First, he was unlucky to see the ball blocked, when a goal looked an absolute certainty, and then he was also in the right spot again, but a downward header from a Heaney cross was brilliantly saved by the Mansfield 'keeper, Ian Bowling.

In amongst all this action, Mansfield had strong claims for a penalty turned down, when Whitley appeared to handle the ball inside the box.

Following the loss of Jamie Pollock, City lost control in the middle of the park and Mansfield looked the likelier and, on fifty-two minutes, they won a penalty when Rimmer pulled down Iyseden Christie in the box. Lee Peacock, a future City signing, smashed the ball into the bottom corner from the spot.

Left: *Cover of programme for City's first and only appearance in the Auto Windscreen Cup.* Right: *A young Nicky Weaver in his playing days for Mansfield.*

Lee Peacock, who later joined City, in action.

Tony Vaughan then gave away a free kick, 30 yards out. Peacock took it and Tommy Wright was left stranded as the ball took a deflection. City were two down – it was hard to believe but it was true. There was still half an hour to play, and City at least pulled one back. When Allsopp raced onto a ball from Danny Tiatto out on the left wing, he drew the 'keeper and fired home.

Manager Joe Royle was disgusted by the performance, but not devastated that City were out of the competition. City's Auto Windscreen challenge had petered out before it had really begun.

Maine Road had witnessed a moment of history that nobody will be telling his or her grandchildren about. The place was in a state of disbelief, but what was more embarrassing: having to compete in the competition, or being knocked out of it at the first attempt? Those who stayed away should count themselves lucky, as the game was unreservedly abject from start to finish, with all the old failings back, notably missed chances and slapdash defending.

City manager Joe Royle's after-match comments: 'Embarrassed and disgusted. The sole saving grace was that were only 3,000 people here to see it, and I apologise to them'.

Manchester City: Wright, Jeff Whitley, Tiatto, Fenton, Rimmer, Vaughan, Brown, Pollock (Jim Whitley), Allsopp, Taylor (Bailey), Heaney
Sub: Crooks

Mansfield Town: Bowling, Ford (Williams), Harper, Peters, Kerr, Hackett (Ryder), Schofield, Christie, Lormor, Peacock, Tallon
Sub: Clarke

Referee: M. Cowburn (Blackpool)

Colchester United v. Manchester City

20 March 1999

Nationwide League Division Two
Layer Road, Colchester
Attendance: 6,554

Colchester United 0   Manchester City 1
                                  Goater

This match was seen as a sign that City were finally overcoming their Division Two stage fright. They had struggled all season to take the lead role in a division packed with teams looking to claim the scalp of a big club.

The Blues went into this game looking for their third double of the season, at one of the less luxurious grounds in the League, which brought home to many of the City travelling army the true reality of how far their club had plummeted.

The excellent pitch appeared perfect for City to play their passing game. Colchester, however, had different ideas and never let City get going. Andy Morrison had to be alert when a Gerard Wiekens back pass fell short, and Colchester went close again when Neil Gregory fired over. The Blues then set out to test 'keeper Carl Emberson, then Shaun Goater had a shot saved following a Terry Cooke cross. Richard Edghill saw a long-range effort go just wide, but for all City's possession the killer touch was missing.

Those seeking entertainment kept themselves busy counting the number of times the ball was cleared over the low stands and out of the ground. City approached the second half in a more confident mood, and Gareth Taylor almost nodded in a Michael Brown cross. Taylor then turned provider to set up Brown, who attempted an audacious chip over the goalkeeper.

The breakthrough finally arrived on fifty-four minutes and a little bit of sporting history was created. A clearance from the Colchester United 'keeper Emberson only reached Cooke in the centre circle. He lifted the ball forward to Goater, who controlled the ball perfectly, bringing it down with his thigh and lobbing it into an empty net. This was the first goal to be ever scored on Sky Box Office's 'Pay-per-view' service.

A couple of minutes later, Taylor had the ball in the net after exchanging passes with Goater, but he was adjudged to be offside. City begun pouring forward, and Brown and Goater were both guilty of wasting chances to wrap up proceedings.

The disallowed goal stung Colchester into action and Warren Aspinall clattered the ball on to the foot of the post, with Nicky Weaver beaten.

The final whistle duly arrived and City were victorious. Although they had not really played well, they went home with the three points. Joe Royle's men were still in the running for an automatic promotion place as the race reached its final lap.

HE WON'T MISS IT, MAKE SURE YOU DON'T

COLCHESTER
v
MAN CITY

FROM 5.30PM SATURDAY 20TH MARCH
YOU CAN WATCH THIS MATCH LIVE AND EXCLUSIVE FOR £7.95 ONLY ON SKY BOX OFFICE

Call the information line on 0990 800 888
Sky Digital customers order using your On-Screen Sky Guide
Cable customers contact your local operator
The match is purchased under Sky's standard terms and conditions for Sky Box Office

ONLY ON
SKY
box office

An advertising leaflet for Sky TV's first ever pay-per-view game.

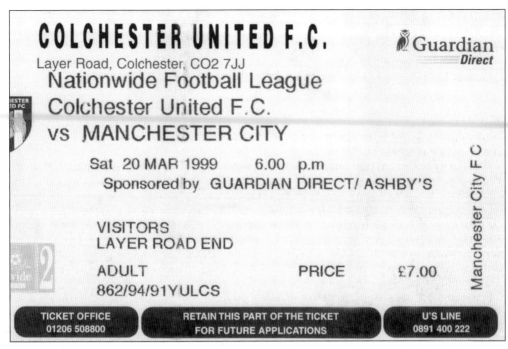

COLCHESTER UNITED F.C.

Layer Road, Colchester, CO2 7JJ

Nationwide Football League
Colchester United F.C.
VS MANCHESTER CITY

Sat 20 MAR 1999   6.00 p.m

Sponsored by GUARDIAN DIRECT/ ASHBY'S

VISITORS
LAYER ROAD END

ADULT   PRICE   £7.00
862/94/91YULCS

| TICKET OFFICE 01206 508800 | RETAIN THIS PART OF THE TICKET FOR FUTURE APPLICATIONS | U'S LINE 0891 400 222 |

Match stub from the all-ticket game. Note the kick-off time.

Manchester City: Weaver, Crooks, Edghill, Wiekens, Morrison, Vaughan, Brown, Bishop, Taylor, Goater, Cooke (Jeff Whitley)
Subs: Dickov, Allsopp

Colchester United: Emberson, Dunne, Duguid, Pounewatchy, Greene, Buckle, Aspinall, D Gregory, Dozzell, N Gregory, Antunes (Sale) (Stamp)
Sub: Williams

Referee: R. Styles (Waterlooville)

City manager Joe Royle's after-match view: 'We ground out a result, but we never really got out of the starting blocks. How often, in the past, have we played well and come away with nothing? I was not very happy with the performance, but we got the points and they could be invaluable'.

Manchester City v. Gillingham

30 May 1999

Nationwide League Second Division Play-Off Final
Wembley, London
Attendance: 76,935

Manchester City 2   Gillingham 2
Horlock, Dickov   *Asaba, R. Taylor*
City won 3-1 on penalties (Horlock, Cooke, Edghill for City, and Hodge for Gillingham).

This must arguably be the most remarkable game in the club's history. For City, it was an opportunity to win at Wembley for the first time in twenty-three years.

The clubs had already met twice during the season. Gillingham gained a creditable no score draw at Maine Road, but went down 0-2 at Priestfield to goals from Kevin Horlock and Terry Cooke. Such was the scramble for tickets for this match that fans were queuing up for twelve hours to get a ticket to see City compete in a one-off winner takes all play-off final.

The Kent side took early control of the game. Guy Butters saw a long-range strike go just wide and when Jeff Whitley slipped, Nick Weaver had to be alert when he tipped over a fierce shot from Mick Galloway. It took a while, but City gradually began to get involved in the game, and Lee Crooks was just inches wide with a strike on goal. A Cooke cross found Kevin Horlock in space, but his header was saved by Vince Bartram.

City had a minor scare on thirty-seven minutes when Carl Asaba scored a goal after he had picked up a Robert Taylor nod-down, but Asaba was adjudged to be offside. Just over the hour mark, City replaced Andy Morrison and Michael Brown with Tony Vaughan and Ian Bishop. Bishop was to supply the cohesion that the tense situation required. Shaun Goater came close with a shot from a narrow angle, which struck the post, and then Cooke had a shot from just outside the area saved well.

Then disaster struck on eighty-one minutes: a Smith through-ball found Asaba in space, and he buried it in the back of the net, rendering the massed City contingent silent. Weaver then tipped a Taylor shot onto the far post, but the Gills were soon two-up. A back-heel from Asaba was picked up by future City signing Taylor, who finished clinically. The Maine Road faithful were stunned, many in the crowd thought it was all over and were making their way to the exits in tears, their dreams shattered.

The next ten minutes defied belief. City pulled a goal back in the last minute, when Goater was tackled on the edge of the box; Horlock stroked the loose ball home to give City some hope. Five minutes of stoppage time were added on, mainly for time-wasting by Gillingham, and Dickov earned himself a place in City folklore when he crashed in a bullet of a right-foot shot with barely seconds left – City were back!

The momentum was now City's, and a result in their favour could be the only

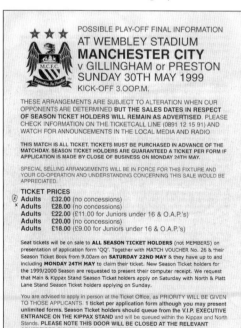

Details of how to get one of 38,000 tickets available to City fans.

outcome from this game. However, chances were few and far between in extra time, and the game had to be decided on penalties. City had a new hero in Weaver, when he saved two of the ensuing penalties.

It was one giant step back to where the Blues belonged, and did City celebrate! It all came right in the end. City goalkeeper Nicky Weaver commented after the match: 'So much has been made about United winning the Treble, we had to give our fans something to celebrate'. Joe Royle said, ' It's a step back to where we should be.'

Manchester City: Weaver, Crooks (G. Taylor), Edghill, Wiekens, Morrison (Vaughan), Horlock, Brown (Bishop), Whitley, Dickov, Goater, Cooke

Gillingham: Bartram, Southall, Ashby, Smith, Butters, Pennock, Patterson (Hodge), Hessenthaler, Asaba (Carr), Galloway (Saunders), R. Taylor

Referee: M. Halsey (Welwyn Garden City)

Season: 1998/99

P	W	D	L	F	A	PTS
46	22	16	8	69	33	82

Division:	Two
Position:	Third
Manager:	Joe Royle
Top Goalscorer:	Shaun Goater (22)
Average Attendance:	24,654

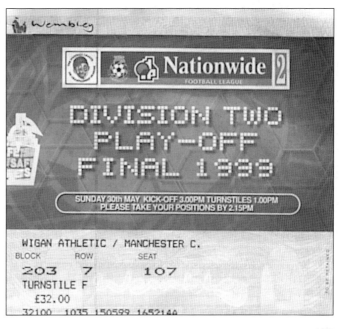

Ticket for the play-off final.

Blackburn Rovers v. Manchester City

7 May 2000

Nationwide League Division One
Ewood Park, Blackburn
Attendance: 29,913

Blackburn Rovers 1   Manchester City 4
Jansen   *Goater, Kennedy, Dickov*
                            Dailly (og)

After what happened with Gillingham in the play-off final, City fans could never have envisaged that they would have another day like it – until this game, that is!

A draw would be enough for City to gain automatic promotion to the Premiership. Surely, the events of this game would not be as dramatic or heart-stopping as those final minutes at Wembley. The scene was set for an emotional roller-coaster of an afternoon.

The game kicked off slightly late, and it was obvious that City were very nervous in the first half, not surprisingly, considering how much was at stake. City just could not gain command of the game and, with half-time only three minutes away, Matt Jansen pounced on Ashley Ward's flick-on from a throw-in. He brought the ball down and volleyed home from near the penalty spot. It was nothing more than Blackburn deserved, especially as Rovers had already struck the woodwork twice.

City had not played well in the first half, so in the second half needed to assert themselves on the game and create more opportunities and, in doing so, brought on Ian Bishop to stamp his authority on the game. Ward than crashed a shot against the angle of the post and bar, straight back into the arms of Nicky Weaver, this was followed Jansen seeing his shot cannon off the foot of the post. Rovers had now struck the woodwork four times. Would City be able to ride their luck for much longer, with them being both outplayed and out thought?

Then, on sixty-one minutes, an equalizer arrived out of nothing. Shaun Goater lay in wait at the far post and converted a Kevin Horlock cross. Minutes later, it was 2-1, as Christian Dailly scored a bizarre own goal. Under pressure from Paul Dickov, he sent a header past the advancing Alan Kelly.

Suddenly it was party time, and City never looked back. More goals were always likely to follow as City got in amongst the Blackburn players and caused all sorts of problems for the two centre halves in particular.

A ball from Jeff Whitley into the Blackburn box caused panic among their defenders, and the subsequent clearance only went as far as Mark Kennedy, who joyfully crashed it in from fully six yards out. He then ran to the City dugout, straight into the arms of his ecstatic manager, Joe Royle.

City were still not finished and, nine minutes from time, another poor clearance by the Blackburn defence was capitalized upon by Dickov. City fans went delirious at the final whistle. It was a great day, one never to be forgotten by those City supporters fortunate enough to get tickets, who turned Ewood Park into the scene of one big blue-

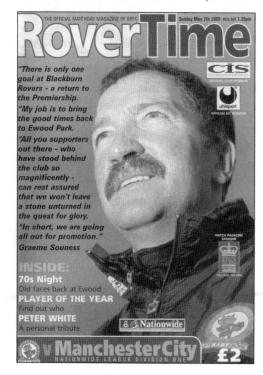

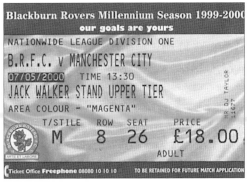

Left: *A ticket rejection: 'Somebody was disappointed.'* Right: *A successful applicant.*

and-white party. City were back where they belonged.

City chairman David Bernstein said, 'Our fans deserve Premier League football. That is the greatest satisfaction'. Top scorer Shaun Goater said, 'I've had a lot of years in the lower divisions. This is what I always wanted'.

Blackburn Rovers: Kelly, Grayson, Dailly, Broomes, Harkness, McAteer, Dunn, Flitcroft, Ward, Jansen, Duff
Subs: Filan (GK), Carsley, Ostenstad, Gillespie, Frandsen

Manchester City: Weaver, Edghill, Tiatto, Prior, Jobson, Pollock (Bishop), Whitley, Horlock, Kennedy (Granville), Taylor (Dickov), Goater
Subs: Wright (GK), Crooks

Referee: T. Heilbron (Newton Aycliffe)

Season: 1999/2000

P	W	D	L	F	A	PTS
46	26	11	9	78	40	89

Division:	One
Position:	Second
Manager:	Joe Royle
Top Goalscorer:	Shaun Goater (29)
Average Attendance:	32,088

Shaun Goater – City's top goalscorer for the last three seasons.

Leeds United v. Manchester City

5 September 2000

FA Premier League
Elland Road
Attendance: 40,055

Leeds United 1	Manchester City 2
Bowyer	Howey, Wiekens

Fans were left to reflect on just how far the Blues had come in the last two years following this 2-1 win over Leeds United. Twenty-four months previously, they had been playing in the Nationwide League Division Two, having sunk to the lowest level in their history, but had then enjoyed successive back-to-back promotions.

After an indifferent start to life in the Premiership, it was widely expected they were in for a hiding against Leeds at Elland Road. The teams had met nine months earlier in an FA Cup tie, which had seen Leeds run out comprehensive 5-2 winners at Maine Road, but Manchester City have an ability to confound the football world and their own fans.

Neither 'keeper was troubled in the opening twenty minutes, but City never surrendered their early initiative, nor was it any great surprise when they went ahead after thirty-four minutes. Paulo Wanchope, who had only arrived back from Costa Rica's World Cup win over Guatemala eight hours before the kick-off, rose to Mark Kennedy's left flank corner and crashed his header against the bar. Steve Howey was first to react, and forced the ball over the line from close range.

Leeds' response was predictably instantaneous, and a shot by Michael Bridges beat Nick Weaver, only to hit the bar. Yet the next goal, in the thirty-seventh minute, came City's way. It followed yet another beautifully flighted corner from Kennedy into the area; Lucas Radebe beat Wanchope to the ball, but Gerard Wiekens chested down the clearance and crashed home

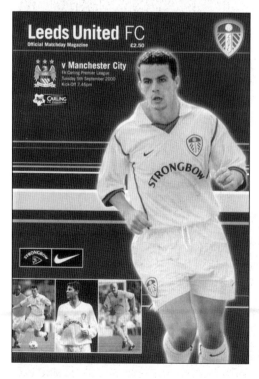

a right-foot volley from the edge of the penalty area that beat Nigel Martyn and went in off the underside of the bar.

More was expected from the home side after the break, and they blitzed City for a good half-hour. The tempo of the match increased when Lee Bowyer headed a goal on fifty-six minutes, following a precise cross from Michael Bridges. That turned out to be the sum of Leeds' efforts, although excellent defence work by Spencer Prior and Norwegian Alfie Haaland contributed to the City goal not being breached again.

City had gone to Elland Road with a game plan and stuck to it superbly. They were now a changed side and showed how much they had progressed. The result was, hopefully, one of the most important in the club's recent history. Heroes could be found all over the pitch and it was a terrific result for the fans who had stuck by them through turbulent times. It was a level that they needed to maintain all season.

City manager Joe Royle's after-match comments: 'It was a tough game and we are very delighted to get the points. Earning three points was a massive boost for all of us. Now we must maintain this level for the rest of the season.'

Leeds United: Martyn, Kelly, Duberry, Radebe, Harte, Jones (Evans), Dacourt, Bowyer, Bridges, Viduka, Smith
Subs: Robinson (GK), Huckerby, Mills, Hay

Manchester City: Weaver, Haaland, Prior, Howey, Ritchie, Jeff Whitley, Wiekens, (Granville), Horlock, Kennedy (Wright-Phillips), Tiatto, Wanchope
Subs: Wright (GK), Dickov, Weah

Referee: G. Poll (Tring)

City's record signing, Paulo Wanchope.

Ipswich Town v. Manchester City

7 May 2001

FA Premier League
Portman Road
7 May 2001
Attendance: 25,005

Ipswich Town 2   Manchester City 1
Holland, Reuser   *Goater*

City entered this game knowing that only victory would give them a chance of survival in their first season back in the Premiership, and even then their destiny would be decided by the last match of season.

Shaun Goater, the club's top goal scorer for the third consecutive season, gave City brief hope on seventy-four minutes when he knocked in a rebound, after Ipswich's 'keeper Richard Wright could only parry Paulo Wanchope's initial shot. Any hopes of a remarkable victory, however, were short-lived, as within the space of ten minutes, a combination of lightning attacks by the Tractor Boys and some poor defending from City saw the trap door to the obscurity of the Nationwide League open.

The players and fans of City entered this game in a positive mood, after a narrow home victory against West Ham in their previous game gave them heart, but they did not take into consideration that Ipswich also had their aspirations. Their opponents wanted to qualify for a place in the League that would give them to chance to play European football the following season.

Ipswich dominated the opening forty-five minutes and, statistically, they had 90 per cent of possession. They pushed City back and limited them to the odd effort on the break. This did not worry City, though, as everything was going accord to the game of not conceding a goal early on, and then gradually becoming more attacking as the game went on. Shaun Goater and

Mark Kennedy were sent on as second-half substitutes to boost City's attacking presence. It was Ipswich, however, who still looked the more likely to score, but, totally against the run of play, Wanchope was inches away from giving City the lead when his overhead-kick hit the foot of a post.

Goater's goal then gave City hope, but the joy did not last and their Premiership dreams ended, as Richard Naylor set up Matt Holland and he fired into the bottom corner from the edge of the area to equalize. When Dutchman Martijn Reuser headed home from two yards, the game, the season and life in the top League ended for City.

The Blues have achieved an enormous amount over the past three years and will surely strive to make an early return to the Premiership.

Ipswich Town: R. Wright, Makin, McGreal, Hreidarsson (Clapham), Bramble, Holland, Magilton, J. Wright (Naylor), Reuser, Armstrong, Scowcroft
Subs: Branagan (GK), Wilnis, Burchill

Two weeks later, Joe Royle was sacked.

Season: 2000/2001

P	W	D	L	F	A	PTS
38	8	10	20	41	65	34

Division:	Premier
Position:	Twentieth
Manager:	Joe Royle
Top Goalscorer:	Shaun Goater (12)
Average Attendance:	34,058

Referee: S. Lodge (Barnsley)

Manchester City: Nash, Charvet, Dunne, Howey, Granville, Tiatto, Whitley, Wiekens, Grant (Goater, Prior), Dickov (Kennedy), Wanchope
Subs: Weaver (GK), Huckerby

The job was mine before Royle went

BY KEVIN AITKEN

KEVIN KEEGAN was named as Manchester City's new manager yesterday – and then revealed he had been approached even before Joe Royle was sacked.

Former boss Royle left on Monday following a brief meeting with chairman David Bernstein but Keegan let slip last night he had been sounded out about the job 24 hours earlier.

He said: 'I had a phone call on Sunday just to see if I would be in any way interested. I was approached on Monday and, by Tuesday afternoon, everything was sorted.'

City director of football Dennis Tueart confirmed: 'We decided over Sunday and I put in a call to Kevin to gauge the depth of interest.'

However, Bernstein insisted: 'The first serious discussions took place on Monday. We sent some people to see Kevin on Tuesday. I was on the phone to him constantly on Tuesday and, by Wednesday night, we had a deal.'

The Blues did not break any rules, however, as Keegan was not with another club, having been out of the game since he quit as England manager in October.

The 50-year-old claims he turned down several offers before signing a five-year contract to become City's ninth manager in 12 years.

And he insisted he was unconcerned by reports of a drinking culture at the club, claiming he was only interested in the future.

'I don't care what happened before,' he said. 'It's a new club for the players. What's gone has gone and I don't know anything about that.

'But I do know one thing, that in the future we will be looking to do everything we can to achieve success.'

I'll awaken sleeping giant: Page 39

Back in the hot seat: Kevin Keegan is all smiles as he is officially unveiled as the new Manchester City manager   Picture Reuters

Football under Kevin Keegan during the 2001/02 season could see an entire new volume of City Classics written.